Que's® Quick Guide to CompuServe®

Mark K. Bilbo

Que's Quick Guide to CompuServe.

Copyright© 1992 by Que® Corporation.

Library of Congress Catalog No: 91-68377

ISBN: 0-88022-825-3

94 93 92   4 3 2 1

Interpretation of the printing code: the rightmost double-digit number is the year of the book's printing; the rightmost single-digit number, the number of the book's printing. For example, a printing code of 92-1 shows that the first printing of the book occurred in 1992.

IBM screens reproduced in this book were created using College Plus from Inner Media, Inc., Hollis, NH.

This book is based on CompuServe Information Services.

Publisher: Lloyd J. Short

Associate Publisher: Rick Ranucci

Product Development Manager: Thomas H. Bennett

Book Designer: Scott Cook

Production Team: Carla Hall-Batton, Claudia Bell, Paula Carroll, Keith Davenport, Brook Farling, Tim Groeling, Carrie Keesling, Bob LaRoche, Laurie Lee, Cindy L. Phipps, Linda Quigley, Sandra Shay, Tina Trettin, Angie Trzepacz, Kelli Widdifield, Christine Young

DEDICATION

To the members of the Native American section of
Issues forum, J.L., R'Dane, Frances, Judy, Bob S., CJ,
and compost pile sitters the continent over.

Product Director

Timothy S. Stanley

Production Editor

Tracy Barr

Editor

Barbara Tilly

Acquisitions Editor

Chris Katsaropoulus

Technical Editor

Tim Ryan

Composed in *ITC Garamond*
and *MCPdigital* by Que Corporation

ABOUT THE AUTHOR

Approximately five years ago, a technical support wizard named Rich West dragged on-line a company named Monogram Software. At the time, Mark K. Bilbo was buried beneath nearly 50,000 lines of Dollars and Sense 4.0 code, which probably explains why he couldn't run fast enough to escape Rich, who was collaring people to be Assistant SYSOPs. Being probably the world's only computer literate neo-Luddite, Mark was immediately bewildered by a world of logons and threads and forums and funny looking symbols that were supposed to be grins.

Yet, Mark got hooked on CompuServe when he discovered he could share his stories of small East Texas towns, Indian reservations, and politics with *thousands* of people. He pulled off his greatest coup when he got Que Corporation to let him write a book to help people understand CompuServe so that they, too, could get hooked, and he even got paid to do it. Is this a great country or what?

TRADEMARK ACKNOWLEDGMENTS

Que Corporation has made every effort to supply trademark information about company names, products, and services mentioned in this book. Trademarks indicated below were derived from various sources. Que Corporation cannot attest to the accuracy of this information.

Apple, Mac, and Macintosh are registered trademarks of Apple Computer, Inc.

AT&T is a registered trademark of AT&T.

CompuServe Information Service is a registered trademark of CompuServe Incorporated and H&R Block, Inc.

IBM is a registered trademark and CIM Advantage is a trademark of International Business Machines Corporation.

Stuffit is a trademark of Aladdin Systems.

Telenet is a registered trademark of GTE Telenet Communications Corporation.

Tymnet is a registered trademark of Tymnet, Inc.

Trademarks of other products mentioned in this book are held by the companies producing them.

ACKNOWLEDGMENTS

A special thanks to Tracy Barr, who edited me into shape and put up with my tendency to talk about everything except the book. To Tim Stanley and Tim Ryan who are both crazy enough to keep coming back for more.

To all the Que Corporation folks who've proven time and again that a company can be big, successful, and *still* filled with just plain, nice folks.

And definitely to Richard D. West who, back in our Monogram Software days, introduced me to that electronic world called CompuServe Information System. I've been hooked ever since and have the monthly bill to prove it. <g>

CONVENTIONS USED IN THIS BOOK

The conventions used in this book have been established to help you learn to use CompuServe quickly and easily. As much as possible, the conventions correspond with those used in the CompuServe Information Services documentation.

CompuServe menu options and commands use the capitalization as shown on the CompuServe screen unless understanding is aided by changing the capitalization in the text. Material that you type is **boldface**; new words and terms that require added emphasis are *italicized*; information that appears on-screen uses a `special` typeface. In addition, money saving tips—denoted by an icon—are added throughout the book to help make using CompuServe as economical as possible.

CONTENTS AT A GLANCE

Table of Contents

Introduction

Science fiction has long toyed with the idea of a large scale computer network that can provide communications and other services by connecting vast numbers of people and machines. For years, we have been able to watch this imagined future become real and have been treated to a world in which enormous amounts of information are literally at our fingertips.

The concept of the global "village" has been with us for some time now. Indeed, because of rapid, electronic communications, the world *is* smaller—prompting some to propose that this interconnection of people and information will bring about enormous changes in the way we work, play, carry out our political processes, and even view our world.

Whether or not the linking of people and machines, combined with the arrival of true "home" computers, will have the predicted effect on our lives remains to be seen. But those of us who were devoted science fiction fans in earlier days and those of us who are just beginning to imagine the possibilities of the electronic age may not be surprised if the predictions come true.

When considering the events of the past week, this author has to admit he is left with an odd feeling of displacement in time. Without leaving his home, he has debated the effect of European colonization of the American continent with people scattered halfway across the globe, researched nationwide databases to discover a grammar book of a relatively unknown Indian language, transmitted the outline of this very book to his publisher, and checked the flight schedules and fares for the intended trip of a friend.

Even as you read this introduction, thousands of people are congregating over the fiber optic cables and copper wires buried beneath your feet and over signals bounced back from space by satellite. They are discussing world events, swapping jokes, playing games, checking the stock market, making business deals, and engaging in numerous activities with people all over the continent and world. Although we may not have yet arrived at the dream of a global network, its beginnings can be seen and used today.

Defining CompuServe

Simply put, computer networks are built by linking machines with phone or other systems and enabling them to share information. The CompuServe Information System (CIS) consists primarily of a group of large, mainframe computers connected to the world by various phone systems. A microcomputer dials a phone number to access a *node* linking it to the mainframes and transmits signals to the mainframes via a modem, which turns information into sound. The mainframes reply in kind, sending the results of the requested operation back. In this way, an individual can access the power of the larger machines to perform operations that far exceed the capacity of the smaller microcomputer.

Although CompuServe is not the only network available, it is the largest and most used of the public systems and offers a wealth of services and activities, a few of which are listed in the following:

■ *CompuServe Mail.* Formerly called EasyPlex, this electronic mail service enables you to send private messages to any CompuServe member. With links to other networks, you also can send electronic mail through MCI Mail, the Internet computer network, any Group 3 fax machine, Telex machines, and even the U.S. Postal Service.

■ *Forums*. These special interest areas enable you to post bulletin-board messages, access numerous files, and communicate on-line with other members who have similar interests. Forum topics range from game playing to software support to literature and beyond.

■ *Research Services*. CompuServe provides numerous research services, but two of the primary ones are the on-line Grolier's Encyclopedia and the IQuest network, which links databases of books in print, magazines, newspapers, dissertations, and so forth.

■ *Shopping*. The Electronic Mall, among other services, is an electronic version of mail-order shopping. You can search for and order books, tapes, clothing, computer software, and many other items; and the number of participating merchants is growing everyday.

■ *Travel Services*. Systems once restricted to travel agents are now available to enable you to search for airline schedules, fares, rental cars, hotel accommodations, and the like. Itinerary planning, reservations, and ticket purchases can now be done on-line from your home.

■ *Financial Services*. Stocks, bonds, securities, indicators, and so forth can be tracked and reported in various ways, bringing Wall Street to the home or office.

Other services exist that enable you to store and retrieve information files, check weather reports, play games, and post nationwide bulletins to find a home for that used computer, bike, or fishing gear that you want to get rid of.

CompuServe Requirements

To access the CompuServe Information Service, you must have the following:

■ *A microcomputer.* No specific type is indicated, though the most popular computers are, of course, the Macintosh and the IBM PC (or IBM clone).

■ *A modem.* To communicate over the phone, a computer must have a modem, which can turn information into sound and sound into information. No particular modem brand is required, and the speed can vary from 300 to 9600 baud. The faster the modem, the more cost effective CompuServe becomes. If you have not yet purchased a modem, consider one that operates at 2400 or 9600 baud.

■ *A CompuServe Membership Kit.* This kit, which is offered through various dealers, bookstores, mail-order companies, or CIS (Customer Service numbers are listed in Chapter 3), includes manuals, quick reference guides, and the CompuServe Information Manager (CIM) communication and interface program (for major computers), as well as instructions for signing on the first time. (CIM is covered in Chapter 11, "Using the CompuServe Information Manager.")

If CIM is not available for your computer or you prefer not to use CIM, you can use any standard telecommunications program. Macintosh users may want to investigate the Navigator program (explained in Chapter 12, "Using Navigator"), while IBM PC and clone users may want to consider TAPCIS (explained in Chapter 13, "Using TAPCIS"). Both programs, which automate many CompuServe operations, can save you money by reducing the amount of time spent on-line with the system.

At this point, one more item is necessary for using CompuServe: money. The following chart reflects CompuServe's current charges:

Baud rate	Dollars per hour
Up to 300	$ 6.00
1200/2400	$12.50
9600	$22.50

Some telecommunications systems you use to access CompuServe may add additional hourly charges. Also, some services (IQuest for example) have additional charges that you are notified of before access.

You can authorize CompuServe to bill your major credit card or electronically draft your checking account. Although the cost has lead some users to (half) jokingly refer to the service as CI$, judicious use can help keep the bill under control, which is one of the ways *Que's Quick Guide to CompuServe* can help. Throughout this book, you can find money-saving tips that enable you to make the best use of your dollars as you use CompuServe.

The Purpose of this Book

With new services being added, naming and explaining the services would result in an enormous book that would be quickly outdated. The purpose of this book, therefore, is not to explain each service in detail, but rather to give you a solid understanding of how CompuServe works. This book is designed to provide needed information and quick reference material to new, intermediate, and experienced CIS users.

This book can give the new user, who may find CompuServe's size and complexity intimidating, a basic understanding of the available services and the necessary, system wide commands.

The user with some CompuServe experience can find tips on using commands and conventions that may not be well documented or explained elsewhere.

All users—even more experienced ones—can benefit from a small, quickly referenced book that pulls together the basics of CompuServe commands and conventions.

The book's format is a cross between reference book and tutorial, presenting the commands and conventions in reference format while also including explanations and examples of their use

CompuServe is first presented from the perspective of the user accessing the service through an ordinary telecommunications package. If CompuServe Information Manager is available to you and you choose to use CIM or another of the automated systems, the menu and information flow control commands may not apply to you; however, the concepts are the same, and understanding the menu system can help you understand CIM, TAPCIS, and Navigator. After all, these programs automate many of the commands discussed in this book. Understanding what the programs are up to can help. Additionally, times may occur when you find yourself facing a CIS command prompt, regardless of the program you use.

Users of these programs may want to compare the sections covering their chosen program to the topic of interest (forums, CompuServe Mail, and so on) as well as read the accompanying manual to understand how to access the service through the program rather than through the CIS menu system.

Logging On to CompuServe

The first step in accessing CompuServe is to *log on*—connect your computer to the computers that make up the service. Your modem must be connected and turned on and your computer's communications package installed and operating. Check the manuals of these items for information on installation.

Because modems have become standardized in recent years, you should have no trouble accessing the CompuServe system with almost any modem on the market. If you do have problems logging on, see Chapter 3, "Getting Help," for the Customer Service number.

The CompuServe Membership Kit contains a list of numbers that you can use to access the service. One of these numbers should be relatively close to you; then, after you log on, you can use the service to locate a number that is best suited to your location.

If you do not find a local number listed and must use a long distance number, using a number farther away may be cheaper. Many times, due to the fierce competition between long distance companies, calling a number serviced by your long distance carrier may be cheaper than calling a number serviced by your regional phone company. Check rates with both companies to see which can give you the better deal.

This may sound odd, but I have found that—due to state regulations—it is cheaper by one-half to call a number outside the state which I live than to call a number in a town only an hour's drive away.

Finally, you must have your User ID and Password before you can log on. A temporary User ID and Password are included in the Membership Kit; you can use these until your account is set up by CompuServe.

Defining Networks

To reach the CompuServe computers, you must access a number that is connected to one of several communications systems. Each network charges a fee for access, usually on an hourly rate. This is added to CompuServe's connect charges.

These networks act as an intermediary between your computer and the CompuServe computers, passing information between them. When possible, access CompuServe through the CompuServe Network, which is, by far, the least expensive. The CompuServe network is available in the U.S., Canada, and Europe, and the numbers that access it are noted both in the Membership Kit and in the online phone listing in Chapter 3, "Getting Help."

If you must access CompuServe through another network, check the hourly rate of the available networks to determine the best price. The available networks are listed in the following and then discussed further in the following sections:

- *CompuServe.* This network, which is the least expensive, is run by CIS and is available in the United States, Canada, and Europe.

- *SprintNet (Telenet).* This network is offered by GTE (owner of U.S. Sprint) and is widely available in the U.S.

- *TYMNET.* This network is provided by McDonnell Douglas is widely available throughout the U.S.

- *LATA (Local Access Transport Area).* This network is provided by the regional Bell system phone companies in the U.S.

- *CSC (Computer Sciences Corporation).* This network, which is available in several countries, enables you to bypass the local phone system.

- *DATAPAC.* This network is provided by Telecom Canada and is available only in Canada.

Accessing CompuServe

If you aren't using CIM, Navigator, or TAPCIS (explained in Chapters 11, 12, and 13), be sure that your communications program is set to 7E1: 7 data bits, Even Parity, and 1 stop bit. Also make sure that the communications program is set to the proper baud rate. For more information about these settings, consult your communication program's manual.

Regardless of the network used, the first step to accessing CompuServe is dialing the phone number. Most communication packages enable you to store a phone number, which you can access through a keyboard command or menu choice. If your communication package offers this capability, select the appropriate option or execute the appropriate command. With other communications packages, you can enter the phone number from the keyboard.

If you have Call Waiting, you should cancel it temporarily to prevent interference with your on-line session (a Call Waiting interruption can break a connection to Compu-Serve). In most areas, you can disconnect Call Waiting temporarily by preceding the number to be dialed with *70. Because *70 is not always used to cancel Call Waiting, however, check with your local phone company.

The phone number entered into your communications package may resemble the following (the commas cause the modem to pause so that, in this example, the command that cancels Call Waiting can be processed):

    *70,,555-1212

When you call from an office phone system, you may need to include the code for an outside line; for example, many office systems require that you dial a 9 before the number. The number entered into your communications package, therefore, may resemble the following:

9,,555-1212

For long distance numbers, of course, you must add a 1 and, possibly, an area code. As a general rule, you can enter into your communications package any numbers you normally dial from your phone, using commas (,) to pause the modem.

Your communications package indicates whether you connected successfully to the network's modem. See the manual that comes with your communications package for an explanation of how a successful connection is indicated. The remaining steps you use to log on are determined by the network you use, as explained in the following sections.

Using the CompuServe Network

After you connect to the CompuServe network, you do the following to log on to CompuServe:

1. Press Ctr+C (hold down the Control key as you press the letter C.) Keep in mind that many Macintosh communications packages use the Command key (⌘) instead of Ctrl.

    If you see the response Host Name:, proceed with step 2; otherwise, skip to step 3.

2. Type **cis** and press the Enter key. (On Macintosh keyboards, press the Return key.)

    The User ID: prompt appears.

3. Type your user ID and press Enter.

    The Password: prompt appears.

4. Type your password and press Enter.

    The CompuServe main menu appears.

Using Sprintnet (Telenet)

After connecting to the Sprintnet network, do the following
to log on to CompuServe:

1. Press the Enter key twice.

   The TERMINAL= prompt appears

2. Type **d1** and press the Enter key.

   An "at" sign prompt (@) appears.

3. Type **c 202202** or **c 614227** and press Enter.

   The User ID: prompt appears.

4. Type your user ID and press Enter.

   The Password: prompt appears.

5. Type your password and press Enter.

   The CompuServe main menu appears.

Using the TYMNET Network

After connecting to the TYMNET network, the following
prompt appears:

   PLEASE TYPE YOUR TERMINAL IDENTIFIER:

Because this prompt is transmitted at 300 baud, it may be
garbled. This is not a problem, continue with the following:

1. Press **A** (do not press Enter).

   The PLEASE LOG IN: prompt appears.

2. Type **cis** and press the Enter key.

   The User ID: prompt appears.

3. Type your user ID and press Enter.

   The Password: prompt appears.

4. Type your password and press Enter.

   The CompuServe main menu appears.

Using a LATA

Although the exact steps in using a LATA may vary, the following steps illustrate the general method of accessing LATAs. Contact the phone company for help if these steps do not enable you to access CompuServe. Alternatively, you can use another network; then check the on-line instructions for the LATA (see Chapter 3, "Getting Help," for more information).

After accessing the LATA, you should see an asterisk (*) prompt. If you do not see the * prompt, type three periods (...). A welcome message appears, followed by the * prompt.

To log on to CompuServe from a LATA, follow these steps:

1. Type **.cps** and press Enter.

2. Type **cis** and press Enter.

   The User ID: prompt appears.

3. Type your user ID and press Enter.

   The Password: prompt appears.

4. Type your password and press Enter.

   The CompuServe main menu appears.

Using the CSC Network

After connecting to the CSC (Computer Sciences Corporation) network, follow these steps to log on to CompuServe:

1. Press Enter several times.

   A # prompt appears.

2. Type **c**.

   A port number, followed by a CENTER prompt, appears.

3. Type **cps** and press Enter.

   The Host Name: prompt appears.

4. Type **cis** and press Enter.

   The User ID: prompt appears.

5. Type your user ID and press Enter.

   The Password: prompt appears.

6. Type your password and press Enter.

   The CompuServe main menu appears.

Using the DataPac Network

After connecting with the DataPac network, log on to CompuServe by following these steps:

1. Depending on your modem—listed in the following—type one, two, or three periods:

110 baud modem	Three periods (...)
300 baud modem	One period (.)
1200 baud modem	Two periods (..)

   A port address that resembles the following (the x's represent numbers) appears:

   DATAPAC: xxxx xxxx

2. Type **compuserve** and press Enter.

   When the connection to CompuServe is made, the following appears:

   DATAPAC: CALL CONNECTED

   If the next prompt is Host Name:, proceed with step 3; otherwise, skip to step 4.

3. Type **cis** and press Enter.

   The User ID: prompt appears.

4. Type your user ID and press Enter.

   The Password: prompt appears.

5. Type your password and press Enter.

   The CompuServe main menu appears.

Locating Phone Numbers

If you log on to CompuServe through a CompuServe network number that is a local phone call, you have little motivation to locate another number because you already are using the least expensive access. If you log on using a long distance number or if you use one of the other networks, however, you may want to locate another access number. In addition, if you plan to use CompuServe while travelling, you may want to locate a number at your destination.

Locating U.S. and Canadian Numbers

To locate a phone number within the U.S. or Canada, do the following:

1. Log on to CompuServe.

   The exclamation mark (!) prompt—the main CompuServe prompt—appears.

   DO THIS!

2. Type **go phones**.

   The menu shown in figure 1.1 appears (the menu options are explained in table 1.1).

3. Type **4** to choose option 4, Search by area code; then press Enter.

   The `Enter area code:` prompt appears.

4. Type the area code and press Enter.

   You are prompted for the baud rate:

   `Enter Baud Rate:`

5. Type the baud rate (**1200,** for example).

   A listing similar to the one shown in figure 1.2 appears.

```
CompuServe (FREE) PHONES


COMPUSERVE NUMBERS
 1 Search by area code
 2 Search by City and State
 3 List all CompuServe Numbers
ALL NETWORK NUMBERS
 4 Search by area code
 5 Search by City and State
 6 List all network numbers
 7 Help and Information
 8 Number changes/additions
```

Fig. 1.1 *The CompuServe (FREE) PHONES menu.*

This listing shows the city, state, network, area code, and phone number of the access numbers that accept the specified baud rate in the specified area code. The networks' abbreviations are listed in the following:

Abbreviations	Network
CS, C, or M	CompuServe network
TYM or T	TYMNET network
TEL or G	Sprintnet (Telenet) network
DPC or D	Datapac network
LAT or L	LATA network

```
CompuServe (FREE) PHONES

City              State Net   AC   Access #
- - - - - - - - - - - - - - - - - - - - - - -
Beaumont          TX    CS M  409  835-0236
Bryan             TX    CS M  409  696-7986
College Station  TX    CS M  409  696-7986
.Conroe           TX    CS M  409  756-8904
Galveston         TX    CS M  409  763-5125
Bryan             TX    TEL   409  822-0159
Nederland         TX    TEL   409  722-3720
Bryan             TX    TYM   409  823-1090
College Station  TX    TYM   409  823-1090
```

Fig. 1.2 The list produced when you search by area code.

If you have a display that is smaller than 80 columns wide, you may see a listing with the single letter network abbreviation following the number.

After viewing the listing of numbers, press Enter to return to the menu shown in figure 1.1. You can search for other phone numbers from this menu.

Table 1.1 CompuServe (FREE) PHONES Menu

Option	Function
1 Search by area code	Searches for CompuServe network numbers only within a specified area code
2 Search by City and State	Searches for CompuServe network numbers in a specified city or state
3 List all CompuServe Numbers	Lists all CompuServe network numbers (not a recommended choice because the listing is very long)

Option	Function
4 Search by area code	Searches within a specified area code for access numbers for all available networks
5 Search by City and State	Searches for all available network numbers in a specified city or state
6 List all network numbers	Lists all available network numbers (not a recommended choice; the listing is even longer than the list created by choosing option 3)
7 Help and Information	Provides information about searching for phone numbers
8 Number changes/additions	Provides information about changes and additions to the phone number listings

Locating Other Numbers

To find access numbers for locations outside of the U.S. and Canada, you choose the Member Assistance option from the TOP menu, which is the first menu displayed when you log on. You also can reach this menu by typing **go top** and pressing Enter.

The Assistance menu appears. Choose option 9, Telephone Access Numbers, by typing **9** and pressing Enter; the NET-WORK ACCESS INFORMATION menu, shown in figure 1.3, appears.

```
CompuServe(FREE)                 LOG-1

NETWORK ACCESS INFORMATION

 1 Telephone Access Numbers

 2 Logon/Logoff Instructions

 3 Node Abbreviations

 4 Busy Signal/Network Problems

 5 Communication Surcharges
```

Fig. 1.3 The NETWORK ACCESS INFORMATION menu.

Choose option 1, Telephone Access Numbers, by typing **1** and pressing Enter. A list of countries and areas appears (see fig. 1.4).

```
CompuServe(FREE)           TELEPHONE

TELEPHONE ACCESS NUMBERS

 1 Africa

 2 Asia and the Pacific Rim

 3 Atlantic/Caribbean Island

 4 Australia/New Zealand

 5 Europe (Eastern)

 6 Europe (Western)

 7 Latin/South America

 8 Middle East

 9 United States/Canada

10 Other

11 800 Direct Dial Access
```

Fig. 1.4 The TELEPHONE ACCESS NUMBERS menu for other countries.

Choose the area from which you want to locate an access number by typing the number to the left of the area (type **7** to locate a number in Latin and South America, for example) and pressing Enter.

The menu corresponding to the area you choose appears. The menu in figure 1.5 displays countries in Latin and South America, for example. Although the menu you access may be different, the principle is the same.

The MORE ! prompt indicates that other countries remain to be listed. To display the rest of the countries, press Enter (see fig. 1.6).

```
CompuServe(FREE)          LOG-305

Latin/South America

1 Argentina

2 Belize

3 Bolivia

4 Brazil

5 Chile

6 Colombia

7 Costa Rica

8 Dominica

9 Ecuador

10 El Salvador

MORE !
```

Fig. 1.5 *A listing of countries from which you can find phone numbers.*

```
CompuServe(FREE)              LOG-306

Latin/South America

11 Guyana

12 Mexico

13 Nicaragua

14 Panama

15 Paraguay

16 Suriname

17 Uruguay

18 Venezuela
```

Fig. 1.6 *The rest of the Latin/South American countries for which you can access numbers.*

Choose the country from which you want to locate an access number by typing the menu number to the left of that country (type **12** for Mexico, for example) and pressing Enter. Depending on the country, you may be presented with a listing of numbers or another menu of cities or perhaps networks. In the example of Mexico, you see a list of the networks through which you can access CompuServe (see fig. 1.7).

```
CompuServe(FREE)              LOG-294

Mexico Access Numbers

 1 Direct Dial

 2 PTT (Public Packet Switching Network)
```

Fig. 1.7 *Options available for accessing CompuServe.*

Choosing one of the networks from the menu presents a menu of cities, as shown in figure 1.8.

```
CompuServe(FREE)          LOG-183

MEXICO - Direct Dial

 1 Cancun

 2 Guadalajara

 3 Hermosillo

 4 Mexico City

 5 Monterrey
```

Fig. 1.8 *A menu of cities.*

From this list, you choose a city by typing the menu number to the left of the city's name (type **2** for Guadalajara, for example) and pressing Enter. The access numbers for the specified city appear (see fig. 1.9).

```
CompuServe(FREE)            LOG-184

GUADALAJARA

  ASYNC  300/2400  (V21)  36-26-0231

  ASYNC  300/2400  (V21)  36-26-0236

  ASYNC  300/2400  (V21)  36-26-0250

  ASYNC  300/2400  (V21)  36-26-0258

  ASYNC 1200/2400  (V22)  36-26-0259

  ASYNC 1200/2400  (V22)  36-26-0337
```

Fig. 1.9 *Phone numbers from Guadalajara.*

Although the exact steps vary from country to country, the principle of using the menus as shown in this section remains the same for all countries.

Changing Your Password

As additional security against others using your account, you should change your password periodically. Your password can be from 8 to 24 characters long and may consist of numbers, letters, and special characters (!, @, and #, for example); in fact, you must use at least one character that is not a letter or number. CompuServe recommends that your password consist of two unrelated words that are separated by a special character. For example (and do not use this one), you may use something like *apple@puppies*. You should not use parts of your name, address, birthdate, or Social Security number as passwords because these can be easily guessed by hackers.

You can change your password at the exclamation prompt (!), which appears when you log on to CIS, with the following steps:

1. Type **go password** and press Enter.

   The following prompt appears:

   ```
   Type your current password:
   ```

2. Type your current password and press Enter.

   The following prompt appears:

   ```
   Now type a new password:
   ```

3. Type your new password and press Enter.

   CompuServe displays the following message:

   ```
   To guard against typing errors,
   Please retype your password:
   ```

4. Type the new password again.

The password changes only if you type the same thing for steps 3 and 4. Neither your old nor new password appears on-screen. In fact, at *no time* will your password appear on-the screen at any legitimate prompt. Also, CompuServe prompts you for your password *only* when you log on and when you change the password with the preceding steps. If prompted for your password at any other time, you should refuse to type it; if the password appears on-screen, do not complete typing it because someone may be trying to trick you into divulging your password.

If you lose your password, call Customer Service so that a new password can be mailed to you. See Chapter 3, "Getting Help," for the Customer Service number.

Setting the User Profile

You use the user profile to inform CompuServe about the specifics of your terminal or communications package. The user profile can help in the display of information. To access the user profile, do the following at the ! prompt:

1. Type **go profile** and press Enter.

   The Change Your User Profile menu appears.

2. Choose the Terminal Settings option by typing **1** and pressing Enter.

   A note informing you whether your permanent and session settings are alike appears; then CompuServe presents you with the Online Terminal Settings menu, shown in figure 1.10.

To understand this menu, you must know that *permanent settings* are settings that apply every time you log on to CompuServe. Despite being called *permanent*, you can change these settings at any time; they are permanent in the sense that CompuServe stores and uses the settings until you change them. *Session settings*, on the other hand, apply only from the time you set them until you log off.

```
1 Instructions
2 Change permanent settings

3 Explanation of session vs. permanent
4 Show session vs. permanent
5 Change session settings

Enter choice!
```

Fig. 1.10 The Online Terminal Settings menu.

The permanent settings should reflect the terminal or communications package you normally use, and you use the
session settings to reflect a terminal or communications
package you are using temporarily—for example, when you
use a friend's computer to log on to CompuServe.

Choosing Permanent Settings

To choose your permanent settings, select the Change
permanent settings option from the Online Terminal Settings menu by typing **2** and pressing Enter. CompuServe
presents the PERMANENT SETTINGS menu, shown in
figure 1.11.

```
PERMANENT SETTINGS

1 Explanation
2 Logon/Service options
3 Display options
4 Terminal type/parameters
5 Transfer protocol/graphic support
6 Make session settings permanent

Enter choice!
```

Fig. 1.11 The PERMANENT SETTINGS menu.

Option 1, Explanation, offers an explanation of permanent settings. The remainder of the options are explained in the following sections.

Logon/Service Options

This option enables you to determine CompuServe's actions when you log on. When you choose this option (by typing **2** and pressing Enter), CompuServe presents the menu shown in figure 1.12 (the settings of your menu may vary).

```
PERMANENT LOGON/SERVICE OPTIONS

1 First service at logon          [MAIN]
2 CompuServe Mail waiting       [NOTIFY]
3 Personal menu established         [NO]
  (Select this to create or
  change a personal menu)
4 TOP goes to                     [MAIN]
5 Online editor                [LINEDIT]
6 Forum presentation mode         [MENU]

Enter choice!
```

Fig. 1.12 *Options that are available when you choose Logon/Service Options.*

The options are explained in the following list:

■ *1 First service at logon.* This option determines which menu CompuServe presents after you log on; [MAIN] indicates the main CompuServe menu. You can change this setting to any service in the CompuServe system.

■ *2 CompuServe Mail waiting.* This option determines what mail message appears when you log on NOTIFY displays a message indicating that mail is waiting. If you select the GO to CompuServe MAIL (GOMAIL) option rather than the NOTIFY option, CIS sends you to the CompuServe Mail menu at log on if mail is waiting.

■ *3 Personal menu established.* You can create your own menu to be displayed at logon; however, this option is beyond the scope of this book and, therefore, not covered. Few users utilize this option after learning CompuServe's GO codes. (See Chapter 2, "CompuServe Basics," for more information about GO codes.)

■ *4 TOP goes to.* This option determines the menu that a GO TOP command sends you to.

■ *5 Online editor.* Two editors are available on CompuServe: LINEDIT and EDIT. Most users find LINEDIT, which uses line numbers, the easiest of the two to use. EDIT does not use line numbers. DEFAULT enables the service to determine which editor to use. Unless you are comfortable with editing text on CompuServe, you should use the LINEDIT option.

■ *6 Forum presentation mode.* This option determines how CompuServe presents forum commands. MENU mode—the mode used in this book—is the easiest to use and presents you with menus each step of the way. The COMMAND mode provides only single word prompts and does not provide menus. Do not use the COMMAND option unless you are very familiar with forum commands. The DEFAULT option expresses no preference for forum command presentation and enables the service to set the method of presentation.

The settings shown in figure 1.5 are recommended for new users; however, you can change any of these options by doing the following:

1. Type the number of the option and press Enter.

   CompuServe displays the option's menu.

2. Type the number of the desired selection and press Enter.

To view the available options without changing the setting, don't type the new number; just press Enter. The setting remains unchanged.

Display Options

You use the display options to conform CompuServe to the type of terminal or communications package you are using. After selecting this option by choosing option 3 from the PERMANENT SETTINGS menu, CompuServe presents a menu similar to the one shown in figure 1.13.

```
PERM DISPLAY OPTIONS

1 PAGED display                    [YES]
2 BRIEF prompts                     [NO]
3 CLEAR screen between pages        [NO]
4 BLANK lines sent                 [YES]
5 Line feeds sent                  [YES]

Enter choice!
```

Fig. 1.13 *The PERM DISPLAY OPTIONS menu.*

The settings shown in figure 1.13 are recommended for new users. The options on this menu are described in the following:

■ *1 PAGED display.* This option determines whether CompuServe pauses between each page of displayed text. To read text as it is sent to your computer, you must set this option to YES. Otherwise, the text scrolls off your screen before you can read it. If you are using a capture buffer, you can set this option to NO and save on-line time by reading the text after you log off.

■ *2 BRIEF prompts.* When set to YES, the prompts issued by CompuServe are shortened. When set to NO, the prompts are longer and easier to understand. A new user who is unfamiliar with the service should choose NO.

■ *3 CLEAR screen between pages.* If set to YES, CompuServe blanks (erases) the screen between pages; if set to NO, the text scrolls continuously. If your communications package has a capture buffer (refer to the manual), you may want to leave this option set to NO and keep a record of your actions on-line. Some communications packages may not understand CompuServe's clear screen command and behave oddly if you set this option to YES.

■ *4 BLANK lines sent.* This option determines whether text is separated by blank lines or not. If set to YES, the text is spaced and easier to read. By setting this option to NO, you can save on-screen space; however, the text may be harder to read. The best setting is probably YES.

■ *5 Line feeds sent.* If your communications package automatically adds a line feed to a carriage return, resulting in text being double-spaced, set this option to NO. Otherwise, set it to YES.

To change any of these options, do the following:

1. Type the number of the option and press Enter.

   CompuServe displays the option's menu.

2. Type the number of the desired selection and press Enter.

   To view the available options without changing the setting, don't choose another option number, simply press Enter. The setting remains unchanged.

Terminal Type/Parameters

The Terminal Type/Parameters settings (option 4 on the PERMANENT SETTINGS menu) conform CompuServe to the communications package that you are using. Communications packages emulate various terminal types and can utilize various control codes. You need to check your communications package manual to determine the emulations and control codes available to you.

When you choose the Terminal Type/Parameters option, CompuServe displays a menu that is similar to the menu shown in figure 1.14.

```
TERMINAL TYPE/PARAMETERS

 1 TERMINAL type                    [VT52]
 2 Screen WIDTH                       [80]
 3 LINES per page                     [24]
 4 Form FEEDS                  [SIMULATED]
 5 Horizontal TABS            [SIMULATED]
 6 Chars. received (CASE)          [U/L]
 7 Chars. sent in CAPS              [NO]
 8 PARITY                          [EVEN]
 9 Output DELAYS                      [0]
10 ERASE when backspacing          [YES]
11 Micro inquiry sequence at logon [YES]


Enter choice!
```

Fig. 1.14 *The TERMINAL TYPE/PARAMETERS menu.*

The options and their appropriate settings are explained in the following list:

■ *1 TERMINAL type.* This option determines the control codes used by CompuServe to send information to your computer. The VT52 and VT100 emulations are widely supported by many communications packages. Other emulations are available, and one should be supported by your communications package. An-Other option is provided in case none of the available options work.

You should not change this setting unless you are experiencing trouble, such as seeing garbled characters on-screen.

■ *2 Screen WIDTH.* This option determines the number of characters your computer can display on one line. This value is usually 80, but it may be less on some systems. Check your computer or communications package manual for the correct setting.

■ *3 LINES per page.* This option determines the number of lines displayed per page. Normally, 24 lines are displayed, but fewer lines may be displayed on older laptops or compact terminals. Check the manual for the correct setting.

■ *4 Form FEEDS.* If your terminal or communications package can respond to the form feed control code, use the REAL setting. Otherwise, use the SIMULATED setting, which is usually the best setting if you are unable to determine whether your communications package accepts form feeds.

■ *5 Horizontal TABS.* As with form feeds, tabs may be created with control characters or by blank space being sent to your communications package. To send the control character, choose REAL; to send spaces, choose SIMULATED, again the best to use if you are uncertain.

■ *6 Chars. received (CASE).* Set this option according to whether your terminal or communications package can receive upper- and lowercase or only uppercase characters. This option is somewhat obsolete because almost all terminals and communication packages can receive both now. Use the U/L setting.

■ *7 Chars. sent in CAPS.* Set this option to NO. If set to YES, all characters, regardless of how you type them, are sent as capital letters, which in CIS "lingo" indicates shouting. Full capitalization is very annoying to other CIS users and makes your messages hard to read.

■ *8 PARITY.* Your terminal or communications package manual should tell you what parity is being used. Set this option to match. Settings are Even, Odd, Zero, None, or One. Change this option only if you are experiencing garbled characters or are instructed to do so by Customer Service personnel.

■ *9 Output DELAYS.* This option causes CompuServe to delay outputs so that your terminal or communication package can "catch up." You should not have to use this option.

■ *10 ERASE when backspacing.* If you set this option to YES—the recommended setting—the characters you backspace over are erased. If you set this option to NO, the characters remain on-screen as you backspace.

■ *11 Micro inquiry sequence at logon.* This option enables CompuServe to "talk" to your communications package at log on. To permit the inquiry, choose YES; to prohibit the inquiry, choose NO. Refer to your software manual to see whether this option is supported.

Transfer Protocol/Graphic Support

The Transfer protocol/graphic support option affects the transfer of files and graphics to and from your computer. You must determine the protocols supported by your communications software before you change these settings. Check your manual for the protocols available to you.

When you choose this option from the PERMANENT SETTINGS menu, you see a menu similar to the one shown in figure 1.15.

```
FILE TRANSFER/GRAPHICS
FILE TRANSFER PROTOCOL
  1 PROTOCOL preference          [SHOW MENU]

GRAPHICS SUPPORT
  2 GIF SUPPORT                        [NO]
  3 NAPLPS SUPPORT                     [NO]
  4 RLE SUPPORT                        [NO]
```

Fig. 1.15 *The options that appear when you choose the Transfer protocol/graphic support option.*

The file transfer protocol options include B Protocol, Quick B Protocol, XMODEM, YMODEM, KERMIT, and A Protocol. XMODEM and YMODEM are perhaps the most widely supported file transfer protocols, but you must check the communication package's manual to determine the best setting for your system.

Quick B is the fastest protocol to use, YMODEM is the next fastest, and XMODEM and Kermit are the slowest. The difference appears in the error checking of each protocol. The faster protocols are more susceptible to phone line noise. If you experience frequent problems with downloading files, you may want to switch to one of the slower protocols; otherwise, use the fastest protocol available to you.

The GIF, NAPLPS, and RLE support options concern different graphics standards. Your communication package manual should tell you which—if any—you may use. Set to YES only the ones your communication software is capable of accepting.

You also can set this option to display a menu before a file transfer occurs (the SHOW MENU setting).

Make Session Settings Permanent

The last option of the PERMANENT SETTINGS menu, Make session settings permanent, enables you to make your session settings permanent. This capability is useful if you make changes during a session and find a combination that works well.

Choosing Session Settings

To set session settings, you can choose the Change session settings option from the Online Terminal Settings menu and then use the same menus as discussed earlier for the permanent settings. Alternatively, you can use SET commands whenever the ! prompt is on-screen. To use SET commands, you type a command in the following syntax:

SET *option setting*

To make the CompuServe prompts brief, for example, type **set brief yes**.

As you may have noticed, the settings menus have some words in the various options in all capital letters, indicating that you can change the option by using the SET command. For example, consider the TERMINAL TYPE/PARAMETERS menu (see fig 1.16).

```
TERMINAL TYPE/PARAMETERS
 1 TERMINAL type                    [VT52]
 2 Screen WIDTH                       [80]
 3 LINES per page                     [24]
 4 Form FEEDS                  [SIMULATED]
 5 Horizontal TABS             [SIMULATED]
 6 Chars. received (CASE)            [U/L]
 7 Chars. sent in CAPS                [NO]
 8 PARITY                           [EVEN]
 9 Output DELAYS                       [0]
10 ERASE when backspacing            [YES]
11 Micro inquiry sequence at logon [YES]


Enter choice!
```

Fig. 1.16 *The TERMINAL TYPE/PARAMETERS menu.*

This menu contains the following words in full capitalization: TERMINAL, WIDTH, LINES, FEEDS, TABS, CASE, CAPS, PARITY, DELAYS, and ERASE. You use the capitalized words in SET commands to indicate and set that option.

Options set in this manner are *session settings*. When you log off, the settings revert to their last permanent setting. To make your session settings permanent, do the following:

1. Type **go profile** and press Enter.

2. Type **1** and press Enter.

3. Type **2** and press Enter.

4. Type **6** and press Enter.

You can get information on the SET command by typing **set help**. You can get even more detailed information by adding an option; SET TERMINAL HELP, for example, lists the available terminal types.

CompuServe Basics

To make the best use of CompuServe, you must understand
how the service is organized. Although a detailed look at the
full service would require a much larger book than this, a
basic outline of CompuServe's organization is explained so
that you can gain an understanding of the available services
and their locations.

Understanding CompuServe Organization

Generally, CompuServe is organized as a linked set of
pages, most of which contain menus offering various
choices. You move from page to page by choosing an option from the menu or using the GO command with the
page name, as explained in the next section, "Navigating
CompuServe."

CompuServe displays the TOP page, shown in figure 2.1,
each time you log on. The menu on this page (referred to as
the TOP menu) acts as your *gateway* into the CompuServe
system.

```
CompuServe                    TOP
   1 Member Assistance (FREE)
   2 Find a Topic (FREE)
   3 Communications/Bulletin Bds.
   4 News/Weather/Sports
   5 Travel
   6 The Electronic MALL/Shopping
   7 Money Matters/Markets
   8 Entertainment/Games
   9 Hobbies/Lifestyles/Education
  10 Reference
  11 Computers/Technology
  12 Business/Other Interests
  Enter choice number!
```

Fig. 2.1 *The TOP page, your gateway to CompuServe.*

Although the TOP menu (like all menus) is subject to change,it probably will not deviate much from the menu shown in figure 2.1. One important thing to note is that the name of the page—TOP—appears in the upper right. The name of each page you encounter as you move through the service appears in this same location. If you find a page that contains items you want to return quickly to, make a note of the page name. Then, by using the GO command, you can move directly to the appropriate page and bypass the menu system.

Another important item you should note is the (FREE) notation next to some of the options. This notation indicates that you can access these areas without being charged by CompuServe (network charges, where applicable, and any long distance charges still accumulate, however). Free areas are always noted with the (FREE) notation.

Each menu choice leads to another page and another menu containing choices related to the selected topic. So that you can gain a basic understanding of the categories, the following list explains the options available on the TOP page:

■ *1 Member Assistance (FREE)*. This option leads to a menu that contains various help options, including locating topics (covered later this chapter), an on-line tour, the Online Today magazine, a summary of commands and instructions, a "What's New" information section, the telephone number location service and user profile options (both covered in Chapter 1), customer service (covered in Chapter 3), and billing information. The name of this page is HELP.

■ *2 Find a Topic (FREE)*. This option, which is covered later in this chapter, offers the capability to search for topics that interest you. The name of this page is INDEX.

■ *3 Communications/Bulletin Bds*. This option presents the communications features of CompuServe and includes the CompuServe Mail system, access to the many forums (covered in Chapter 4), the national bulletin board (covered in Chapter 11), and the public file areas (covered in Chapter 10). The name of this page is COMMUNICATE.

■ *4 News/Weather/Sports*. This option consists of the news and weather services of CompuServe, including the AP Online service, Newsgrid, weather reports (discussed in Chapter 11), and so forth. The name of this page is NEWS.

■ *5 Travel*. This option contains the travel services, discussed in Chapter 8. Through this menu, you can access airline schedules, hotel accommodations, itinerary planning, rental cars, tours and cruises, as well as forums relating to travel and leisure. The name of this page is TRAVEL.

■ *6 The Electronic MALL/Shopping*. Through this option, you access the Electronic Mall—a large gathering of vendors—and other shopping services, covered in Chapter 7. The name of this page is SHOPPING.

■ *7 Money Matters/Markets*. This option accesses a menu that contains various financial services and forums, explained in Chapter 9. You use this option to access stock quotes, investment information, company information, and so on. The name of this page is MONEY.

■ *8 Entertainment/Games.* The many games available through CompuServe are listed on the menu that you access through this option. The name of this page is GAMES.

■ *9 Hobbies/Lifestyles/Education.* This "catch all" category covers personal finance, health and fitness, hobbies, art, and so forth. The name of this page is HOME.

■ *10 Reference.* This option contains the reference services of CompuServe. You can access Groiler's Encyclopedia and IQuest, as well as other reference services, through this option. The name of this page is REFERENCE.

■ *11 Computers/Technology.* This option covers the many hardware and software related forums on CompuServe, electronic magazines and news services geared toward computers, as well as software and hardware merchants. The name of this page is COMPUTERS.

■ *12 Business/Other Interests.* This option includes various professional forums and services for business management, engineering, legal, health, and so on. The name of this page is BUSINESS.

Although this listing is by no means comprehensive, it should give you a basic idea of the categories of services that CompuServe offers.

Navigating CompuServe

You can move around the CompuServe system in two ways: using the menus or using the GO command. To use the first method, you make selections from the various menus, starting from the TOP menu and progressing downward until you locate the desired area. Although using menus is the easiest method, it is also more time-consuming and, thus, more expensive.

The faster method is using the GO command and the Quick Reference Word. After you learn the Quick Reference Word for an area of interest, you can use the GO command to move directly to that area, bypassing the menus.

Using the Menus

Using the menus is very simple. When CompuServe presents a menu, you are prompted with Enter choice! or a similar prompt. The exclamation mark (!), indicates that CompuServe is waiting for a command. To make a menu selection, do the following:

1. Type the number of the menu choice.

2. Press Enter. CompuServe displays the next menu or the service you selected. (You also can use various commands, listed in table 2.1, at the ! prompt.)

Table 2.1 Commands at the Exclamation Prompt

Command	Function
B	Display preceding page
F	Display next page (pressing Enter normally does the same)
H and ?	Display help text
M	Return to preceding menu
N	Display next item on menu (if you choose option 1,typing N displays option 2)
P	Display preceding item on menu (if you choose option 2, typing N displays option 1)
R	Redisplay the current page (good when noise on the phone line garbles the information)
T	Return to the TOP menu
OFF	Log off of CompuServe

If a prompt other than the ! prompt (such as a : or > symbol) appears, you must place a slash (/) before the command. Although some commands may not work at such prompts, the Help command should work at all times.

Using GO Commands

The GO command is the quickest way of moving from page to page within the CompuServe system. As stated earlier, every page has a name—called the *page identifier* or *quick reference word*. As you move around in the CompuServe system, carefully watch the upper right of the screen. You can see the name (which appears in uppercase and sometimes consists of numbers as well as letters) change from page to page. As you find areas of interest, note the page name; then when you want to go directly to a page, do the following at the ! prompt:

1. Type **go** and the page name.

2. Press Enter.

CompuServe transfers you to the specified page. To return to the TOP menu, for example, type **go top** and press Enter.

Note that the *CompuServe Quick Reference* booklet in your Membership Kit contains a list of the forums and services and the corresponding quick reference words (or page identifiers). You can get on-line help finding quick reference words by using the Find a Topic service (option 2 in the TOP menu), which you access by using the GO INDEX command, explained later in this chapter.

Controlling Information Flow

Several keyboard commands are available to help control the way CompuServe displays information on your computer. To execute these commands, press the Control key (Ctrl) as you press the specified letter or symbol. Table 2.2 explains these keyboard commands. *Note:* If you use a Macintosh, you press the Command key (⌘).

Table 2.2 Keyboard Commands

Command	Result
Ctrl+C	Cancels the operation being performed and displays a menu that asks if you need help, want to go to the TOP menu, or move to the preceding menu.
Ctrl+O	Cancels the flow of text to the screen. Use this command if you don't want to continue reading an article or notice. A prompt appears, and you can issue a new command.
Ctrl+S	Halts the flow of information to the screen so that you can read it before it scrolls off.
Ctrl+Q	Resumes the flow of information to the screen. Use this command to proceed through the information that you stopped by pressing Ctrl+S.
Ctrl+U	Deletes typing. This code erases everything you typed since the last time you pressed Enter. Press Ctrl+U to erase a mistyped command.
Ctrl+V	Retypes the line. This code retypes everything you typed since the last time you pressed Enter and is very useful when you use the CB simulator or a conference area in a forum because messages from other users tend to overlap your typing.

Finding Topics

To locate a topic, you can use the Find a Topic index, which enables you to enter a word or phrase and responds with a list of CompuServe areas that contain the specified topic. You also can obtain a complete list of all available topics, which takes some time to complete.

To access the index, do the following:

1. At the TOP menu, type **2** to choose the Find a Topic option; then press Enter. Alternatively, type **go index** and press Enter.

   The menu shown in figure 2.2 appears.

```
CompuServe Index (FREE)     INDEX
FIND A TOPIC
  1 Search for Topics of Interest
  2 List ALL Indexed Topics
  3 Explanation of Index
Enter choice!
```

Fig. 2.2 *The INDEX menu.*

2. To search for a particular topic, type **1** to choose the Search for Topics of Interest option; then press Enter.

   The following prompt appears:

   ```
   Enter topic (e.g. stock) :
   ```

3. Type the desired topic (for example, type **macintosh** or **ibm pc**) and press Enter.

   A list of topics similar to the one shown in figure 2.3 appears.

```
ALDUS Forum                         ALDUS
Adobe Forum                         ADOBE
Aldus Customer Service Forum        ALDSVC
Aldus/Silicon Beach Forum           SBSALDFORUM
Apple News Clips($)                 APPLENEWS
Enter GO PAGE!
```

Fig. 2.3 A list of topics produced using the INDEX menu.

The name of the service or forum appears on the left. To the right is the quick reference word. The Enter GO PAGE! prompt enables you to enter the name of a page you want to go to. Alternatively, pressing Enter causes the INDEX menu to reappear so that you can perform another search.

Getting Help

Several ways exist to get help when using CompuServe. So that you can understand and use commands easily, help is available at nearly every prompt. CompuServe provides a Customer Service department proven to be responsive and helpful both on-line and over the phone. A practice forum that is free of connect time (though network charges still apply) is also available so that you can ask questions as you practice using forum commands. This chapter covers one of the more mundane aspects of obtaining help: checking to see just how much money you're spending.

Using On-line Command Help

At any exclamation mark prompt (!), you can type **help** to acquire an on-line summary of the commands that are valid at that prompt. Other prompts, such as : or **>**, require that you precede the Help command with a slash (/)—type **/h** or **/help**, for example.

In many areas, such as forums, the on-line help provides a list of commands. You type the name of the command for which you want more help.

Using On-line Customer Service

Before sending a message to customer service, you may want to check the Questions and Answers section where many frequently asked questions have been answered. If the Questions and Answers section doesn't include your question, you can easily compose and send it to Customer Service through Feedback.

To access on-line Customer Service, type **go questions** at any ! prompt. (Remember, other prompts may require a slash (/) before the GO command.) A menu similar to the one shown in figure 3.1 appears.

```
ASK CUSTOMER SERVICE
  1 Questions and Answers
  2 Feedback
  3 Contacting Customer Service
  4 Mentor Training Seminars
Enter choice!
```

Fig. 3.1 The ASK CUSTOMER SERVICE menu.

Questions and Answers

To access Questions and Answers, select option 1, Questions and Answers, from the ASK CUSTOMER SERVICE menu or type **go oqa-6** at any ! prompt. (Other prompts may require that a slash (/) precede the GO command.) A QUESTIONS AND ANSWERS menu, similar to the one shown in figure 3.2, appears.

Pressing Enter produces more categories (you can use the B command to return to the preceding menu). Enter the number that corresponds most closely to the subject of your question.

```
QUESTIONS AND ANSWERS
 1 Billing
 2 Logon/System Access
 3 CompuServe Mail/MCI Mail
 4 Forums
 5 Personal File Area
 6 First Service/Personal Menu
 7 Executive Option
 8 CompuServe's Online Ordering
   Service
 9 CB Simulator
10 Market Quotes
Enter choice or (CR) for more!
```

Fig. 3.2 *The QUESTIONS AND ANSWERS menu.*

When you choose an option from the QUESTIONS AND ANSWERS menu, CompuServe displays another menu that lists the various questions in the chosen category. If the prompt reads or (CR) for more!, more questions and answers are available and can be accessed by pressing the Enter key. To move back one set of questions, use the B command.

Feedback

Feedback enables you to ask questions or make comments on-line to Customer Service. You receive the answers to your questions through CompuServe Mail. To access Feedback, choose option 2, Feedback, from the ASK CUSTOMER SERVICE menu; then press Enter. Alternatively, type **go feedback**.

A menu of question categories appears. Choose the category that your question corresponds to by entering the number of the category and pressing Enter. If none of the categories seem to fit, use the Other category. You may be asked to provide additional information, such as the type of computer you are using. Type the appropriate information and press Enter.

CompuServe prompts you to type your letter to Customer
Service. Type each line, pressing Enter at the end. When
you finish the letter, type /exit at the beginning of a new
line and press Enter. A menu of options regarding your
letter appears (see fig. 3.3).

```
Message processing
You may now:
  1 - Send the message
  2 - Edit the message
  3 - Type the message
  4 - Erase the message
```

Fig. 3.3 *The menu that appears when you complete your letter to Customer Service.*

To send the message to Customer Service, type **1** and press
Enter. If you change your mind, choose option 4, Erase the
message, by typing **4** and pressing Enter. Option 3, Type
the message, enables you to view the message before taking
further action.

To edit the message, type **2** and press Enter. The EDIT
menu shown in figure 3.4 appears.

```
CompuServe                EDIT
  1 - CHANGE characters in line
  2 - REPLACE line
  3 - DELETE line
  4 - INSERT new line(s)
  5 - TYPE all lines
  6 - LIST selected lines
  0 - Exit editing
```

Fig.3.4 *The EDIT menu.*

To review your letter, choose option 5, TYPE all lines, which causes CompuServe to print your letter on-screen. To replace a line, choose option 2, REPLACE line. CompuServe asks you for the line number, which you enter by typing the number and pressing Enter. Then you type the new line. To delete a line, choose option 3, DELETE line; then type the line number and press Enter.

Changing characters is only a bit more complicated. After you choose option 1, CHANGE characters in line, CompuServe asks you for the line number (use option 5, TYPE all lines, to see the lines and their numbers). CompuServe types the current line and prompts you for the *string* (a group of characters) to be replaced. Type in the characters that you want to replace. After you enter the string, CompuServe prompts you for the new string. An example of this procedure is shown in figure 3.5.

```
Which line #: 2
Current line:
2: and legged on through the Shreveport
   node. I found that
Text to replace: legged
Replacement text: logged
New line:
2: and logged on through the Shreveport
   node. I found that
```

Fig. 3.5 *Editing text in CompuServe.*

To end editing, choose option 0, Exit editing, and press Enter. CompuServe returns you to the message processing menu from which you can send the message.

Calling Customer Service

Times may occur when you need to communicate with Customer Service by phone. Obviously, if you are experiencing trouble logging on to CompuServe or have lost your password, you cannot use the on-line Feedback system.

Customer Service representatives are available from 8 A.M. to midnight weekdays and from 2 P.M. to 10 P.M. weekends, Eastern time. Holiday hours, as well as service hours outside the U.S., may vary. In the United States, the Customer Service number is 1-800-848-8990. Outside the U.S., you can use the following numbers:

Country	Customer Service Number
United Kingdom	0800-289-458
UK from elsewhere in Europe	(44)(272)255-111
Germany	0130-4643
Switzerland	155 31 79
Other European countries	(49)(89) 66 55 0-222

You should have handy your user ID and a detailed description of the problem.

Using the Practice Forum

CompuServe can be confusing for beginners. Learning the appropriate commands can be a time-consuming task and an expensive lesson. Fortunately, CompuServe provides a Practice Forum, which is free of connect charges. Although network charges (such as for Telenet or Sprintnet) still apply, CompuServe waives the regular hourly connect charge while you use the Practice Forum. In addition, the Practice Forum SYSOPs (SYStem OPerators, those who oversee a forum) can answer your questions about CompuServe and assist you in learning to use the system.

To save money as you learn how to use CompuServe, use the Practice Forum. When you use the Practice Forum, CIS waives regular connect charges so that you can practice using CompuServe and ask questions of the SYSOPs without worrying about the cost.

To enter the Practice Forum, type **go practice** at the ! prompt, which appears after you log on. A welcome message followed by the forum menu appears (see fig. 3.6).

```
PRACTICE Forum Forum Menu
 1 INSTRUCTIONS
 2 MESSAGES
 3 LIBRARIES (Files)
 4 CONFERENCING (0 participating)
 5 ANNOUNCEMENTS from sysop
 6 MEMBER directory
 7 OPTIONS for this forum
 8 JOIN this forum
Enter choice !
```

Fig. 3.6 *The PRACTICE Forum Forum Menu.*

Because you can do little if you are not a member, you should join the forum immediately. To join the forum, type **8** to choose the Join this forum option; then press Enter. CompuServe prompts you for your name (see fig. 3.7).

```
Please enter your name: Mark K. Bilbo
Mark K. Bilbo
Is this correct (Y or N)? y
Inserting name and ID...
```

Fig.3.7 *The prompt that appears when you join the Practice Forum.*

CompuServe may display an announcement to inform you of recent changes or topics that may be of interest to you. The forum menu appears again; this time, however, the option to join the forum (which you have done) no longer appears.

Joining a forum does not usually incur extra charges. A dollar sign ($) indicates any option that costs more than the usual connect charges; therefore, before you choose an option, you know that it may cost extra.

At this point, you can use the forum to practice your skills or to ask questions about CompuServe. Chapter 4, "Using Forums," covers the forum commands.

Checking Your Billing

You may want to determine exactly how much money you're spending by using CompuServe. You also may want to change billing information, such as your address. To access the billing menu, type **go billing** at the ! prompt. The BILLING INFORMATION menu appears (see fig. 3.8).

```
CompuServe(FREE)          BILLING
BILLING INFORMATION
  1 Current Rates
  2 Review Your Charges
  3 Electronic Funds Transfer (EFT)
      (U.S. Addresses Only)
  4 Billing Options Explained
  5 Changing Your Billing Address
  6 Update Billing Information
  7 Executive Service Option
  8 General Billing Information
```

Fig.3.8 The BILLING INFORMATION menu.

The options of this menu are explained in the following:

- *1 Current Rates.* This option displays a menu that enables you to check the CompuServe rates. You can check the hourly connection charges in the U.S. and other countries, the charges for using various networks to access CompuServe (such as Sprintnet), and so on.

- *2 Review Your Charges.* This option enables you to determine how much money you have spent using CompuServe and is covered in more detail later in this section.

- *3 Electronic Funds Transfer.* This option enables you to change options connected with the EFT billing option, which permits CompuServe to bill your bank account automatically.

- *4 Billing Options Explained.* This option provides an explanation of the billing options and instructions regarding how to select one.

- *5 Changing Your Billing Address.* This option enables you to change your address and phone number.

- *6 Update Billing Information.* This option enables you to change your billing information, such as checking account number, credit card number, or other method of payment.

- *7 Executive Service Option.* This option enables you to sign up for the Executive Service which—in exchange for a higher monthly payment—lets you access more special services, some with discounts.

- *8 General Billing Information.* This option gives you general information concerning CIS billing and various packages available.

Option 2, Review Your Charges, is the option you use to check the amount of money you have spent using CompuServe. Type **2** and press Enter; a menu similar to the menu shown in figure 3.9 appears.

```
CompuServe (FREE) CHARGES
 1 Explanation
 2 Account Balance
 3 Billing History
USAGE DETAILS
 4 Current activity
 5 Previous activity
 6 Mail Hardcopy ($)
Enter Choice !
```

Fig. 3.9. The menu that appears when you choose option 2, Review Your Charges.

These options are explained in the following sections. The (FREE) notation indicates that you are not charged for the connect time while you use the options of this menu. Network charges continue to accumulate, however.

Getting Your Account Balance

Choosing option 2, Account Balance, from the CompuServe CHARGES menu produces information regarding your account balance (see fig. 3.10).

The items in this report are explained in the following:

- *Balance.* Displays the balance from the previous week. Although billing occurs once a month, CIS updates billing information about once a week. The balance is the total of the charges since the last payment but not including the current activity.

- *Activity since.* The various items listed below this heading total the activity of the current week since the date indicated (in figure 3.10, since December 28, 1991, for example).

- *Payments.* This item indicates the total of payments since the indicated date.

- *Charges.* This item indicates the total connect charges and other charges since the indicated date.

```
              ACCOUNT BALANCE
   Balance as of 12/28/91     $73.86
    Activity since 12/28/91:
     Payments                  -.00
     Charges                 $63.72
     Credits                  -1.26
     Adjustments               .00
                            --------
    Balance as of 1/11/92   $136.32
                            ========
   Account limit: $300.00
   Last Payment: 12/16/91
```

Fig. 3.10 *Account balance information.*

- *Credits.* This item lists credits that CompuServe issues for various reasons. Your use of free services and bonuses (periodically, CompuServe offers bonuses for using services, such as the Electronic Mall) are credited here.

- *Adjustments.* Other accounting adjustments are recorded here. If you do not understand the adjustment, contact Customer Service for an explanation.

- *Balance as of.* This item indicates the current total of charges. This information may lag a day or two behind, that is, it may not include the activity from the past day or two.

- *Account limit.* This item displays the monthly limit of your account. The account limit is similar to a credit limit. CompuServe can adjust this limit if necessary (the request must be made by calling Customer Service). When you reach your account limit, CompuServe may temporarily suspend your account unless you arrange for a payment to be made or have the limit raised by calling Customer Service.

- *Last payment.* This item indicates the date of your last payment to CompuServe.

When you finish viewing the listing, press the Enter key to return to the CompuServe CHARGES menu.

Checking Your Billing History

Option 3 of the CompuServe CHARGES menu, Billing History, displays a listing of your account's billing history for about the past three months, as shown in figure 3.11.

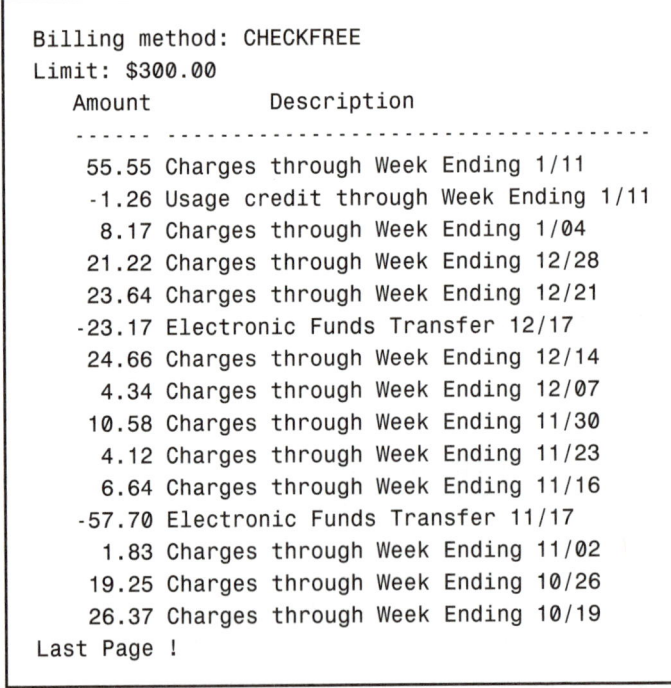

```
Billing method: CHECKFREE
Limit: $300.00
   Amount         Description
   ------  -------------------------------------
    55.55 Charges through Week Ending 1/11
    -1.26 Usage credit through Week Ending 1/11
     8.17 Charges through Week Ending 1/04
    21.22 Charges through Week Ending 12/28
    23.64 Charges through Week Ending 12/21
   -23.17 Electronic Funds Transfer 12/17
    24.66 Charges through Week Ending 12/14
     4.34 Charges through Week Ending 12/07
    10.58 Charges through Week Ending 11/30
     4.12 Charges through Week Ending 11/23
     6.64 Charges through Week Ending 11/16
   -57.70 Electronic Funds Transfer 11/17
     1.83 Charges through Week Ending 11/02
    19.25 Charges through Week Ending 10/26
    26.37 Charges through Week Ending 10/19
Last Page !
```

Fig. 3.11 An example of a billing history.

The items in figure 3.11 are explained in the following:

■ *Billing method.* This item indicates which method you chose for your CompuServe billing. Checkfree is the EFT method in which your bank account or credit card is charged automatically.

■ *Limit.* This item displays the account limit.

■ *Amount.* The amount of each charge (indicated by a positive number) and each credit (indicated by a negative number) are listed below this heading.

■ *Description.* The purpose of each charge or credit is listed here.

■ *Usage credit through Week Ending.* Usage credits usually reflect the time you use free services, which CompuServe may charge against your account but then credit. Other credits may be earned in special offers.

■ *Charges through Week Ending.* This indicates the total of charges for the specified week.

■ *Electronic Funds Transfer.* If you use the Checkfree option, this item indicates a payment made by charging your checking account. Other payment options indicate payments in a slightly different way.

Other notations may appear from time to time. If you do not understand a notation, call Customer Service or use Feedback to ask about the notation. When you are finished, press Enter to display the CompuServe CHARGES menu again.

Checking Your Current Activity

Option 4 of the CompuServe CHARGES menu, Current Activity, shows a detailed listing of your most recent activity. You may not always have a current activity record, however, because at the end of each week, the current activity record moves into the previous activity records of option 5 (discussed in the following section). In other words, you start each week with a "blank slate." You may receive the message No charge information found when you choose option 4. This message indicates that you need to check previous activity for your charge information. Recording your most recent activity may take a day or two.

After choosing option 4, CompuServe provides billing information, as shown in figure 3.12.

```
                  BILLING DETAIL (Page 1 of 1)
     Date  Description              Node   Logon  Min Amount
     ----- ----------------------  ------  -----  --- ------
     01/11 ORDER #    704616                          12.55
           SHIPPING   704616                          15.00
           STD CONNECT-2400 BAUD 07SVP  23:23    6    1.25
           CPS NETWORK SURCHARGE                 6     .03
           TOTAL FOR SESSION                          1.28
     01/10 STD CONNECT-2400 BAUD 09LCH   0:15    1     .21
           CPS NETWORK SURCHARGE                 1     .01
           TOTAL FOR SESSION                           .22
           STD CONNECT-2400 BAUD 06LCH   0:16    3     .62
           FREE SERVICES                         2     .00
           ONLINE ORDER CR                       5     .00
           FREE SERVICES                         1     .00
           CPS NETWORK SURCHARGE                11     .06
           TOTAL FOR SESSION                           .68
           STD CONNECT-2400 BAUD 06LCH  20:24    4     .83
           FREE SERVICES                         1     .00
           CPS NETWORK SURCHARGE                 5     .03
           TOTAL FOR SESSION                           .86
           STD CONNECT-2400 BAUD 06LCH  20:58    3     .63
           CPS NETWORK SURCHARGE                 3     .02
           TOTAL FOR SESSION                           .65
           SALES TAX                                  3.19
```

Fig. 3.12 *Billing information provided by CompuServe.*

Consider the first charge record:

```
STD CONNECT-2400 BAUD 07SVP  23:23 6  1.25
CPS NETWORK SURCHARGE              6   .03
TOTAL FOR SESSION                     1.28
```

This record, which is typical of CompuServe charge records, consists of the following:

Record Item	Description
STD CONNECT	Indicates the kind of connection. Formerly, CompuServe charged a different standard and prime time rate. Now CIS charges a single rate (determined by modem speed) regardless of the time of day you log on. Although you may occasionally see *PRI CONNECT*, the rate is the same as STD CONNECT.
2400 BAUD	Indicates the baud rate you use. CompuServe charges different rates based on the speed of your modem.
07SVP	Indicates the connection node. The code is generally an abbreviation for the city in which the node is located.
23:23	The time, displayed in 24-hour format, that you logged on to CompuServe. (13:00 is 1 P.M., 14:00 is 2 P.M., and so on to 23:00 which is 11 P.M. Midnight is expressed as 0:00.)
6	The number of minutes you were logged on.
1.25	The connect charge for the time you spent on CompuServe.
CPS NETWORK SURCHARGE	Indicates the charge for the network you used to log on to CompuServe. CPS is the CompuServe network. You may see other notations for different networks. (Again, 6 is the number of minutes you were logged on, and the number to the far right is the amount you were charged.)
TOTAL FOR SESSION	Indicates the total charge for the session—the time between log on and log off.

You may see other notations. In states that charge sales tax on communications, for example, you may see a SALES TAX notation. If you place an order with CompuServe, you may see a notation similar to the following:

```
ORDER #   704616              12.55
SHIPPING  704616              15.00
```

This information indicates the order number and the amount of the item or items. The shipping is noted on a separate line.

Part of the Jan. 10 record includes the following:

```
STD CONNECT-2400 BAUD 06LCH   0:16  3    .62
FREE SERVICES                       2    .00
ONLINE ORDER CR                     5    .00
FREE SERVICES                       1    .00
CPS NETWORK SURCHARGE              11    .06
TOTAL FOR SESSION                        .68
```

In addition to the usual items, you see FREE SERVICES and ONLINE ORDER CR. CompuServe includes these items, which concern free services, primarily to note your usage. CompuServe doesn't charge you for the time listed (notice the .00 to the right of each item). The total time logged on was 11 minutes, as displayed by the CPS network surcharge. Three minutes were spent using parts of CompuServe; therefore, CIS includes a connect charge. The remaining 8 minutes were spent using free services.

Other notations may appear from time to time. If you do not understand a particular notation, contact Customer Service.

When you are finished viewing your records, press Enter to return to the CompuServe CHARGES menu.

Checking Your Previous Activity

At the end of each week, CompuServe transfers your current activity record to the previous activity section. You can then access the activity records through option 5 of the

CompuServe CHARGES menu, Previous Activity. Type **5** and press Enter; a menu similar to the one shown in figure 3.13 appears.

```
CompuServe (FREE) CHARGES
    Week Ending        Total
    - - - - - - - - - -    - - - - -
 1    Jan-11-92        $44.29
 2    Jan-04-92        $38.17
 3    Dec-28-91        $21.22
 4    Dec-21-91        $23.64
 5    Dec-14-91        $24.66
 6    Dec-07-91        $24.34
 7    Nov-30-91        $10.58
 8    Nov-23-91        $34.12
 9    Nov-16-91        $26.64
10    Nov-02-91        $21.83
11    Oct-26-91        $19.25
Enter choice !
```

Fig. 3.13 *A record of previous activity.*

CompuServe retains your records for about three months. You can access the detail of each week by choosing the corresponding number. To see the usage of the week ending January 11, 1992, for example, type **1** and press Enter. CompuServe displays a detailed listing of the current activity record. The previous section explains this listing.

Press Enter at this menu to display the CompuServe CHARGES menu again.

Using Other Options

Option 1 of the CompuServe CHARGES menu, Explanations, displays an explanation of the menu's options. Option 6, Mail Hardcopy ($), enables you to request a print-out of your billing records. A dollar sign ($) appears next to option 6, indicating that you incur additional charges when you choose this option. Each print out of a week's activity you request costs a nominal fee.

Using Forums

Forums, which are the most popular—and perhaps the most addictive—aspect of CompuServe, are essentially electronic meeting places for people with similar interests. A forum is a specialized section of CompuServe that has its own theme. Literally hundreds of forums exist; for instance, you can find forums entitled ISSUES and IBM on CompuServe. Lively debates and discussions occur in forums throughout CompuServe in both the message board and the conference areas. Forum libraries, which contain files submitted by members, can be valuable sources of information, software, or entertainment.

Although each forum has different rules and conventions, most are open and friendly. You should never fear joining in. This chapter gives you an overview of how forums work, as well as the rules and conventions common to all forums.

Forum Basics

This section covers the forum basics: what forums are, how to find a forum that interests you, how to join the forum, and conventions in reading and leaving messages in the forum.

As stated earlier, forums serve as a meeting place for people with similar interests. Forums consist of three primary parts: the *message area*, which acts as a kind of electronic bulletin board; the *conference room*, which enables members to have real time conversations, similar to telephone conferencing except that the comments are typed rather than spoken; and the *libraries*, which contain various files submitted by members.

Forum activity is overseen by SYSOPs or system operators. The job of the SYSOP, who may have assistants aiding him or her, is to maintain the forum, assist users, and enforce the rules of CompuServe. If you have a question, feel free to ask a SYSOP.

Finding a Forum

With the number of available forums, finding a forum that interests you can be difficult. Many users of CompuServe note that even if they know of one or two forums that interest them, the other forums remain a mystery. Still, finding a forum is actually quite easy: you can simply use the TOP menu, which appears when you log on to CompuServe (see fig. 4.1).

```
CompuServe                    TOP

  1 Member Assistance (FREE)
  2 Find a Topic (FREE)
  3 Communications/Bulletin Bds.
  4 News/Weather/Sports
  5 Travel
  6 The Electronic MALL/Shopping
  7 Money Matters/Markets
  8 Entertainment/Games
  9 Hobbies/Lifestyles/Education
 10 Reference
 11 Computers/Technology
 12 Business/Other Interests
 !
```

Fig. 4.1 The TOP menu.

Option 2, Find a Topic, gives you access to the forum index. After you type 2 and press Enter, the FIND A TOPIC menu, shown in figure 4.2, appears.

```
CompuServe Index (FREE)   INDEX
FIND A TOPIC
 1 Search for Topics of Interest
 2 List ALL Indexed Topics
 3 Explanation of Index
 !
```

Fig. 4.2 *The FIND A TOPIC menu.*

You can use the FIND A TOPIC menu's option 2, List ALL Indexed Topics, to obtain a listing of all forums; however, the listing is extensive, and you incur network charges as CompuServe produces the listing. An easier—and less expensive—way to list topics is to use option 1, Search for Topics of Interest.

Suppose, for example, that you are interested in finding a forum where issues relating to Native Americans are discussed. Rather than searching through the entire forum list (which appears when you choose option 2), you can choose option 1, Search for Topics of Interest. When you choose option 1, CompuServe displays a prompt asking for the topic. At the prompt, type **native americans** and press Enter. CompuServe responds with a list, similar to the one shown in figure 4.3, of forums (if any) that are indexed to that topic. In this example, only one forum—the Issues forum—is indexed to your topic.

```
Enter topic (e.g. stock) : Native Americans
Issues Forum                ISSUESFORUM
Enter GO PAGE!
```

Fig. 4.3 *The list of forums indexed to the Native Americans topic.*

To the left is the name of the forum (Issues Forum), to the right is the GO code (or page name), ISSUESFORUM. To reach this forum, you type **go issuesforum**. (Although listed in all capital letters, you can enter the GO code and page name in upper- or lowercase.)

To search for another topic, press Enter at the Enter GO PAGE! prompt; CompuServe returns you to the FIND A TOPIC menu. Choose option 1 again and proceed as before.

You use option 3, Explanation of Index, of the FIND A TOPIC menu to obtain an explanation of the topic index.

Joining a Forum

After locating a forum of interest, you can proceed to that forum by typing **go** *forum* (where *forum* is the GO code for the forum) at any ! (exclamation mark) prompt. You then see the visitor announcement, which gives you a brief overview of the forum, including the name and CIS number of the SYSOP. This information is followed by the Forum Menu. The menu for the Foreign Language forum, which is a typical forum menu, is shown in figure 4.4.

```
FOREIGN LANGUAGE Forum Forum Menu
 1 INSTRUCTIONS
 2 MESSAGES
 3 LIBRARIES (Files)
 4 CONFERENCING (0 participating)
 5 ANNOUNCEMENTS from SYSOP
 6 MEMBER directory
 7 OPTIONS for this forum
 8 JOIN this forum
Enter choice !
```

Fig. 4.4 A typical forum menu.

Being a visitor, you have only limited access to the forum. You can view the instructions for the forum (option 1), read the announcements (option 5), or join the forum (option 8). The most interesting parts of the forum (such as options 2 through 4) are unavailable to visitors.

Because option 8, JOIN this forum, has no dollar sign ($) to the right of it, you know that joining the forum costs no more than the usual connect charges. You should not hesitate to join because joining places you under no obligations. To join the forum, type **8** and press Enter. CompuServe prompts you for your name, as illustrated in figure 4.5.

```
Please enter your name: Mark K. Bilbo
Mark K. Bilbo
Is this correct (Y or N)? y
Inserting name and ID...
Thank You For Joining FOREIGN LANGUAGE Forum !
Press <CR> !
```

Fig. 4.5 *Joining a forum.*

The Press <CR> ! prompt indicates that you must press the Enter key before CIS displays more information. After you press Enter, forum announcements usually appear. These announcements are posted by the SYSOP to inform you of special events, discussions, or files present in the forum. If you see something of interest, make a note of it.

You are now a member of the forum and ready to begin exploring. One of the best places to start is the message area.

Introducing Yourself

Traditionally, newcomers to a forum introduce themselves if they intend to participate in the message area discussions; however, introducing yourself is not a requirement. You can read messages, for instance, even though you may never leave a message. In CIS terms, this activity is referred to as *lurking.* Although its name makes lurking sound a bit

devious, it is perfectly acceptable. No one will chide you for
failure to participate nor chase you from the forum if you
decide merely to listen in.

Despite the connotations of the word, lurking has a
definite place in the on-line community. Should you be
interested in a topic but not feel comfortable enough to
comment, you can read along as the experts discuss it. You
also can lurk about a forum, watching the types of discussions going on to decide if you want to participate. In any
case, forums are public places and, after all, you are paying
to use the service! Feel free to lurk as you please.

Reading messages is covered in the section "Using the
Message Area" in this chapter. If you want to lurk before
introducing yourself, skip to the following section "Understanding Forum Conventions"; then proceed to "Using the
Message Area."

You gain the most benefit from a forum by participating.
When you decide to participate, you can introduce yourself
to the forum members by following these steps:

1. From the Forum Menu (refer to fig. 4.4), choose
   option 2, MESSAGES.

   The Forum Messages Menu appears (see fig. 4.6).

```
The Issues Forum Messages Menu
Message age selection = [New]
  1 SELECT (Read by section and subject)
  2 READ or search messages
  3 CHANGE age selection
  4 COMPOSE a message
  5 UPLOAD a message
Enter choice !
```

Fig. 4.6 The Forum Messages Menu.

2. Choose option 4, COMPOSE a message.

The editor that enables you to compose messages appears and prompts you for the first line of your message:

```
The Issues Forum Compose
Enter message. (/EXIT when done)
  1:
```

3. Type the first line of the message. The line should be no more than 80 characters. As a rule of thumb, press Enter when the line almost reaches the right side of your screen.

Each time you press Enter, another line number appears. Repeat step 3 until your message is complete. Try to keep the message short. You can enter a blank line by pressing Enter at the line number prompt.

4. Type /**exit** and press Enter.

A sample hello message is shown in figure 4.7.

```
The Issues Forum Compose
Enter message. (/EXIT when done)
  1: Hello. I'm new to the forum and wanted
      to introduce myself.
  2: I live in the Texas area and wondered
      if there are Native
  3:    American events in my area.
  4:
  5: J.W.
  6: /exit
```

Fig. 4.7 *A sample hello message.*

Entering /exit informs the editor that you have finished entering the message, and the forum Post Action Menu appears (see fig. 4.8).

```
The Issues Forum Post Action Menu
1 POST message on board
2 EDIT message
3 TYPE message
4 MAIL via CompuServe Mail
5 CANCEL message compose
Enter choice !
```

Fig. 4.8 *The Post Action Menu.*

Choose option 1, POST message on board, to *post* the
message, that is, place the message on the message board.
When you post a message, CompuServe prompts you for a
receiver and subject:

```
Post for (Name and/or User ID): All

Subject: Native American events
```

By typing **all** after the Post For prompt, you indicate that
the message can be received by all who search for messages
on the message board. Usually a message is posted to a specific individual. You can post a message to the SYSOP by
typing **sysop** after the Post For prompt. If you want the
message to be read only by the SYSOP, type ***sysop***.

After entering the recipient of the message, CompuServe
prompts you for the subject, which should be a short summary of the topic of your message. Typing **hello, new-
comer**, **new to forum**, or something similar is good. If you
are asking a question (as in the example), a brief summary
of the question's topic is acceptable. You also can edit the
message. For instructions on editing a message, see the
next section, "Editing Messages."

Press Enter to enter the subject. CompuServe asks for the
section in which the message is to be posted. Each forum is
divided into sections, creating a *topic list*. The messages
are divided by topic within the general topic of the forum.
You see a listing of the sections, as shown in figure 4.9.

```
Section # Required
 1 Around the World
 2 Political Issues
 3 Individual Liberty
 4 New Democrats
 5 Between the Sexes
 6 Parenting Issues
 7 Defense-War&Peace
 8 Selfhelp & Handicap
 9 Rush H. Limbaugh
10 Paranormal Issues
11 Native Americans
12 Men's Issues
13 Marginal Issues
14 Seniors
15 Ethics/Human Rights
16 Adoption Today
17 Lesbian/Gay Issues
Enter choice !
```

Fig. 4.9 *A topic list.*

Enter the number of the section that is closest to the subject of your message. If you are entering a general hello message, enter the number of the section you are most interested in. To post the example message in section 11, Native Americans, you type **11** and press Enter. A confirmation appears (see fig. 4.10).

```
To: All
Subj: Native American events
Section: 11
Is this correct (Y or N)?
```

Fig. 4.10 *A confirmation that appears when you post a message.*

Type **Y** and press Enter to confirm your posting, subject, and section entries. To make a change, type **N** and press Enter; CompuServe prompts you for information again. After confirming your entries, the message number appears:

```
Message # 223008 posted

Press <CR> !
```

The message number depends on the forum and how many messages were posted before yours. You rarely have to worry about message numbers, which are used in only a few commands (such as the DELETE Message command), and you can find the message number after you post the message by using the READ command. The message number appears in all message headers.

Depending on the forum, a day or so after you post your message, you should receive replies. Some replies will be simple welcomes, others will be more introductory, and others may ask about your interests or answer questions that you asked. The section "Using the Message Area" explains how to tell whether your message has received a response, how to retrieve your messages, and how to respond to the replies.

Editing Messages

In "Introducing Yourself," you saw how to compose and post messages. You also should know how to edit a message before posting it. After you type /**exit**, which indicates that your message is complete, the Post Action Menu appears (refer to fig. 4.8).

Option 2, EDIT message, is your key to editing the message. Before you use option 2, however, use option 3, TYPE message, to determine whether your message needs editing. When you choose option 3, your message appears on-screen so that you can check for errors. If no flaws are present, you can post the message by choosing option 1, POST message on board. If you see errors to be corrected, however, choose option 2 to display the Edit Menu (see fig. 4.11).

```
The Issues Forum Edit Menu
 1 CHANGE characters in line
 2 REPLACE line
 3 DELETE line
 4 INSERT new line(s)
 5 TYPE all lines
 6 POST message on board
 7 MAIL via CompuServe Mail
Enter choice !
```

Fig. 4.11 *The Edit Menu.*

To replace a word or phrase in a line, choose option 1,
CHANGE characters in line. CompuServe prompts you for
the line number. (As explained earlier, you see the line
numbers when you choose the TYPE option from the Post
Action Menu; you also can choose option 5, TYPE all lines,
from the Edit Menu to display the line numbers.) After you
enter the appropriate line number, CompuServe displays
the specified line and prompts you for the characters to be
replaced and the characters that are to replace them, as
shown in figure 4.12.

```
Which line #: 1
Current line:
1: wondering if anyone knows of Natavo
   American events in this area.
Text to replace : Natavo
Replacement text: Native
1: wondering if anyone knows of Native
   American events in this area.
Okay? Y
```

Fig. 4.12 *Replacing a word or phrase in a line.*

The corrected line appears, and CompuServe asks you to
confirm the change. Type **Y** for yes, **N** for no.

To replace an entire line, use option 2, REPLACE line. CompuServe prompts you for the line to replace and then prompts you to type the new line (see fig. 4.13).

```
Which line #: 3
Current line:
3: In the catalog, it says that it is. Are
   you sure? I thought
Type in replacement:
Are you sure that it doesn't work with
   System 7? I was under the
Line # 3 replaced
```

Fig. 4.13 Replacing an entire line.

To delete a line, use option 3, DELETE line. CompuServe prompts you for the number of the line to be deleted.

To insert lines, use option 4, INSERT new line(s). CompuServe prompts you for the number of the line that the inserted lines should follow. Enter 0 to insert lines at the beginning of the message. When you insert lines, you must type **/exit** when you finish, as shown in figure 4.14; otherwise, CIS assumes you want to insert more lines.

```
Insert after which line (0 if at top): 0
 1: Hi there! I was wondering if you could
    tell me about
 2: /exit
```

Fig. 4.14 Typing /exit when you are finished inserting lines.

You use option 5, TYPE all lines, to review the entire message. If you are ready to post it, you use option 6, POST message on board, or option 7, MAIL via CompuServe Mail.

To return to the Post Action Menu, which contains the option to cancel the message altogether, press Enter without typing an option number.

Understanding Forum Conventions

When you post written messages, the normal body language and expressions that accompany speech are absent. A wry comment is usually accompanied by a slight smile. But how can you smile in writing? Without the smile, your comment may be misinterpreted as sarcasm.

One of the most typical mistakes that newcomers make is the use of uppercase letters. In CIS convention, uppercase words are the equivalent of raising your voice. In fact, over time, many frequent users complain that a message using uppercase letters actually "sounds" like shouting. Consider the following three versions of the same sentence, for example:

Let me tell you what I really think.

Let me tell you what I REALLY think.

LET ME TELL YOU WHAT I REALLY THINK.

As you read these, you may notice that the *really* in the second sentence gives the impression that the speaker's voice is being raised. This version is the equivalent of verbally saying "Listen you, let me tell you what I REALLY think"— something you might want to do only if you are really steamed. The third sentence, which is unacceptable on the forums, comes across as if the speaker were shouting in a small room. Although writing in full capitalization is not against the rules, it is likely to cause comments from other users asking you to stop shouting.

A more acceptable way to emphasize a word or idea is to use an asterisk (*) before and after the word or to indicate underlining with an underscore mark (_) before and after the word, as in the following examples:

Let me tell you what I *really* think.

Let me tell you what I _really_ think.

These softer versions emphasize that the comments are
your true opinion but do not give the reader the impression that you are angry. Because the written word can be
easily misinterpreted in the absence of facial expressions,
gestures, and tone of voice, you should stick to the less
strident versions.

Other conventions have arisen to express facial expressions, such as smiles. These symbols—called *emoticons* for
emotional icon—are usually typed at the end of a line or
message to indicate the sender's intent. If you're having
trouble deciphering an emoticon, tilt your head to the side
and look at it again. The most commonly seen emoticons
are listed in table 4.1.

Table 4.1 Common Emoticons

Emoticon	Expression
<g>	Grin
:) and :-)	Smile
:-o	Surprise
:-(	Frown
:-I	Hmm
:-x and :-#	My lips are sealed
;-)	Wink

Only the smile and grin emoticons are seen on a regular
basis. A whole host of emoticons exist but are not widely
used. If you encounter an unfamiliar one, keep in mind
that many are made as if the head of the person is tilted
to the left—the colon (:) creates the eyes, the dash (-)
the nose, and the other symbols the mouth. Viewing the
emoticon with this in mind may help you recognize
the implied facial expression.

Many users have developed their own style for implying
facial expressions. You may see such things as the
following:

That's what *you* think. <smirk>

He said that? *chortle* *choke* You CAN'T be serious!

There are few hard and fast rules to indicate facial expressions, laughter, and the like. Over time, you can see how others express these emotions and most likely will develop your own style.

Additionally, because messages must be brief, a whole host of abbreviations has arisen. You should know these abbreviations so that you can understand messages on the board, as well as abbreviate your own messages. The abbreviations used to shorten messages express common statements. Some abbreviations are fairly obvious; others can be difficult to figure out. Table 4.2 lists the common abbreviations.

Table 4.2 Common Abbreviations

Abbreviation	Stands for
BRB	Be right back (used mainly in conferencing)
BTW	By the way
CI$	CompuServe (a reference to spending too much money using the system)
CIS	CompuServe
CO	Conference; on-line, interactive discussions with other users.
FWIW	For what it's worth
FYI	For your information
gr&d	Grinning, running, and ducking (often used after a particularly bad joke)

continues

Table 4.2 Continued

Abbreviation	Stands for
IAE	In any event
IMO	In my opinion
IMHO	In my humble opinion
IOW	In other words
OIC	Oh, I see
OTOH	On the other hand
ROF,L	Rolling on the floor, laughing (in reply to a particularly funny comment)
RSN	Real soon now

The following sentences illustrate how these abbreviations can be used:

OTOH, System 7 can be slow if you try to...

BTW, did you see the new printer...

IMHO, the movie was a waste of money.

He said the package would be released RSN.

With the number of messages involved in a discussion, the number of people replying, and the days that can separate logons, remembering exactly what you wrote in an earlier session can be difficult. A message replying to a comment made a week ago can leave a user scratching his head, trying to remember the content of his last message.

To solve this problem, a convention has arisen in which the comment being replied to is bracketed by less than and greater than signs (>><<) or surrounded by quotes and used in the reply message. Consider the following message from Joe:

Message: #150623, S/12 Political Issues

Date: Wed, Jan 8, 1992 23:42:20

Subject: President's trip

From: Joe Dobransky

To: J. W. Langsford

Give me a break here! He drags a bunch of auto executives along to whine to the Japanese over imports, throws up at a state dinner, then comes home claiming he's created jobs, jobs, jobs?

The man hasn't done a blasted thing to protect American industry. The trip was all show.

Joe

Message: #150634, S/12 Political Issues

Now consider J.W.'s response:

Date: Fri, Jan 10, 1992 8:32:15

Subject: President's trip

From: J. W. Langsford

To: Joe Dobransky

>>...throws up at a state dinner...<<

Don't tell me *you're* going to start into this too. It's as if the President isn't allowed to get sick.

>>The trip was all show.<<

Maybe so. But at least he isn't proposing starting a trade war that will throw the country into a depression. The last thing we need is to slow the economy down with protectionist measures that'll only benefit rich car company executives.

J.W.

Quoting a portion of the message not only clarifies the part of the message being replied to, but it also helps "jog" the recipient's memory so that he does not have to reread the old message. Keep in mind that a message can be left on Wednesday, replied to on Friday, and the reply read on Sunday—four days after the message was composed.

Some users prefer using the initials of the person quoted, as shown in figure 4.15, especially if more than one person is being replied to in the same message, assuming all the users are reading along (messages cannot be sent to more than one person at a time).

```
Message: #5063, S/14  Software
   Date:    Tue, Dec 19, 1991 23:42:20
   Subject: Zippercom
   From:    Joe Dobransky
   To:      J. W. Langsford
JW: The package is a complete waste of money.
I junked it and bought Fastbits. Haven't
looked back yet.
TN: ...then lost the entire file! I was
afraid it would go after my hard drive next.
I don't know what's going on here. I've used
the program for the past year without a
problem. You sure something else isn't con-
flicting with it?
Joe
```

Fig. 4.15 *Using initials of the users who sent the messages being replied to.*

With time, you can discover the best combinations of abbreviations, emoticons, and quoting conventions for you. Use this section as your guide to deciphering the messages of others and saving some time—and, therefore, money—in your use of CI$.

Reading Forum Announcements

Announcements are posted by the SYSOP to inform you of
special events, new files in the libraries, or a particularly
interesting discussion occurring on the message board.
Announcements also are used to publicize important information about CompuServe, such as rate changes, forum
command changes, and so forth.

The most important announcements appear automatically
when you first enter a forum. As you have seen, a visitor
announcement appears when you enter a forum that
you haven't joined. After you become a member, new
announcements appear automatically when you enter
the forum.

You can access these announcements, as well as announcements not automatically displayed, by choosing option 5,
ANNOUNCEMENTS from SYSOP, from a Forum Menu.
Figure 4.16 shows the Issues Forum Menu, which is typical
of other forum menus. Choosing option 5 from this menu
produces the Forum Announcements Menu, shown in
figure 4.17.

```
ISSUES Forum Forum Menu
 1 INSTRUCTIONS
 2 MESSAGES
 3 LIBRARIES (Files)
 4 CONFERENCING (0 participating)
 5 ANNOUNCEMENTS from SYSOP
 6 MEMBER directory
 7 OPTIONS for this forum
```

Fig. 4.16 A typical forum menu.

```
The Issues Forum Announcements Menu
 1 News flash
 2 General
 3 Messages
 4 Conference
 5 Library
 6 Membership
 7 SYSOP roster
Enter choice !
```

Fig. 4.17 *The Issues Forum Announcements Menu.*

The following explains the announcement categories of the Issues Forum Announcements Menu:

- *1 News flash.* This option includes a "what's new" type of announcement that you normally see the first time you enter a forum. Because news flashes do not automatically appear after the first time you see the newest announcement, this option enables you to review the news flash in case you missed reading it the first time.

- *2 General.* This option, which includes general information about the forum, usually appears the first time you enter a forum; however, it also is available for later review.

- *3 Messages.* This option includes information about the message area and any forum specific instructions (such as whether any of the forum sections are *closed* and how you can apply to use them).

- *4 Conference.* This option contains information about on-line conferencing and conference (commonly called CO) schedules.

- *5 Library.* This option includes general information about the libraries of the forum.

- *6 Membership.* This option includes information about being a member of the forum. Few forums have special requirements for membership; those that do detail the requirements here.

- *7 SYSOP roster.* This option includes a list of the people who run the forum and are available to assist you, the user IDs of the SYSOPs, and information about divisions of responsibility, if applicable to the forum.

After you read an announcement, press Enter to return to the Announcement Menu. Pressing Enter again returns you to the Forum Menu.

Using the Message Area

The message area is the heart of the forum. In this area, users leave messages for one another on the various topics with which the forum is concerned. This section explores the organization of the message area, the available commands, and strategies for use.

Understanding the Message Area

The message area, which is similar to the *BBS*—Bulletin Board System—that has been popular in computing for some time, is something of a cross between mail and a bulletin board. Messages, usually addressed to one person (although many people can read them), are *posted* on the board. Perhaps the closest noncomputer parallel is the Letters to the Editor column of a newspaper. In such a column, the messages may be addressed to a single individual (usually the editor or another letter writer), but they are read by many who, in turn, can respond. Unlike the limitations of the Letters to the Editor column, the message area has room for hundreds of messages, which can be made available immediately.

To use the message area effectively, you need to understand its basic organization, the topic of the next sections.

Sections

Because of the volume of messages contained in a forum, CIS divides messages into separate sections, each relating to a different topic within the forum. Sections are numbered from 0 to 17. (Zero is usually reserved for SYSOP use and not generally available.) At least one section (usually section 1) in each forum is devoted to general topics about the forum. This is the section you use for messages asking about the forum itself or seeking help.

The Literary Forum (Litforum), for example, is broken down into sections such as Fiction (section 6), Non-fiction/tech (technical writing—section 12), Market Maneuvers (marketing information—section 2), Journalism (section 5), and so forth. Messages are posted according to the topic they most closely concern. By categorizing the topics, CIS enables you to narrow down the messages to be searched and, consequently, eliminate the subtopics in which you are not interested.

Some sections are *closed*; you must request permission to access them. Generally, closed sections are special interest sections that the SYSOPs need to control more closely than the other sections. The Literary Forum, for example, holds writing classes in a closed section. The SYSOPs will open a section to you after you discuss your interest with them. You then can post and read messages in that section. The message announcement (discussed in an earlier section) informs you of the existence and conditions of closed sections.

Sections divide the forum topic into subtopics. A further division involves the subject heading of the messages themselves, as explained in the next section.

Subject Headings

Within each section, messages have *subject headings*. The first user to post a message determines the subject, entering it as shown in the introductory message used earlier in this chapter. Replies to the message and replies to the replies use the same subject heading. You can obtain a listing of the subject headings within a section, as explained in the section "Selecting a Message Thread." Viewing the subject headings can help you further narrow your search for messages of interest.

In many forums, subject headings change from time to time. Because of the growing volume of messages and the tendency of the message exchange to drift from one topic to another, SYSOPs rename messages to reflect the topic more accurately. Not all forums do this, however; the SYSOPs determine whether to change subject headings. But if you follow a discussion and see the subject heading change, the SYSOP has more than likely changed the heading.

So far, you have seen that a forum has a broad topic, that message sections divide the forum into subtopics, and that subject headings further divide it. You may have a mental image of a plant root—a single thread at top breaking into sections which, in turn, break into subject headings. This is a useful image to keep in mind in the following discussion about threads.

Threads

In the Literary Forum, you may decide to post a message asking whether Dave Barry, the Florida humorist, has another book out. You place the message in section 8, Comics & Humor, with a subject *New Dave Barry??*

When you next enter the forum, you find that the message has three replies. One asks if you seriously think Dave Barry is funny, another lists the latest books he has written that the respondent knows about, and one simply asks who Dave Barry is. Here you have started a new *thread*. At the top is your message asking about a new Dave Barry book. Linked to your message are three replies, all of which retain your subject heading.

You respond to each of the three. You tell the first respondent that, yes, you think Dave Barry is funny and perhaps mention a newspaper column or two you liked. To the other respondent, you relate that you own the books listed and had heard that another was forthcoming. To the last, you explain that Dave Barry is a columnist who lives in Florida and has several books out.

When you next enter the forum, you find that your one message has started off a chain of messages and replies. Several people have joined in on the discussion with the first respondent to offer their opinions of Dave Barry. The second yields one or two replies about the book title that is forthcoming and a query asking whether you have read other humorists. The third has touched off a discussion about Florida and Southern humor.

As you can see, threads can get both interesting and confusing and may take some getting used to. Keeping the "root" image in mind can help, however. Figure 4.18 is a very simplified diagram of the thread structure.

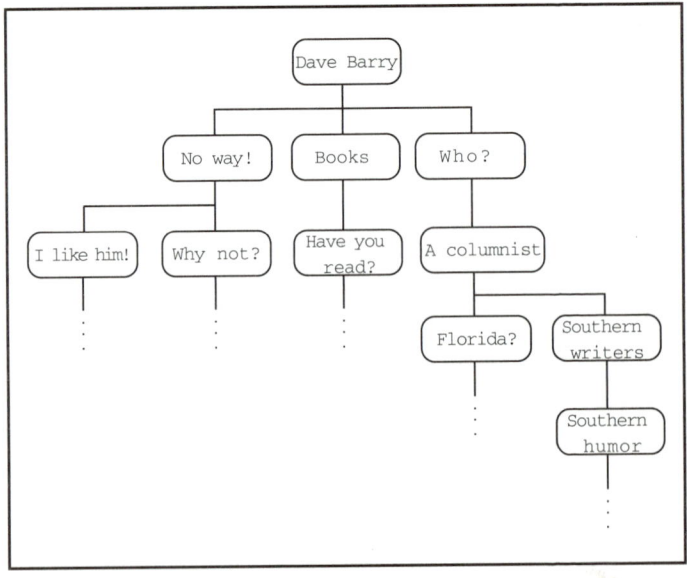

Fig. 4.18 A simplified thread structure.

Fortunately, CompuServe organizes things so that you can follow the thread in a way that mimics conversation. How you do this is covered in the sections "Selecting a Message Thread" and "Following a Message Thread" of this chapter.

Accessing the Message Area

When you first enter a forum, you are presented with the
Forum Menu (see fig. 4.19).

```
Literary Forum Forum Menu
 1 INSTRUCTIONS
 2 MESSAGES
 3 LIBRARIES (Files)
 4 CONFERENCING (0 participating)
 5 ANNOUNCEMENTS from SYSOP
 6 MEMBER directory
 7 OPTIONS for this forum
```

Fig. 4.19 *A Forum Menu.*

The only command related to the message area is option 2,
MESSAGES, which enables you to enter the message area.
Type **2** and press Enter. The Messages Menu, which you
use to select a message thread, appears (see fig. 4.20).

```
The Literary Forum Messages Menu
Message age selection = [New]
 1 SELECT (Read by section and subject)
 2 READ or search messages
 3 CHANGE age selection
 4 COMPOSE a message
 5 UPLOAD a message
Enter choice !
```

Fig. 4.20 *The Literary Forum Messages Menu.*

Selecting a Message Thread

Choosing option 1, SELECT, from the Forum Messages
Menu produces a Sections Menu from which you can select
a message thread (see fig. 4.21).

```
The Literary Forum Sections Menu
Section names (#subjs/# msgs)
 1 General/Help  (10/25)
 2 Market Maneuvers  (2/5)
 3 Resolutions for '92  (1/1)
 5 Journalism  (1/3)
 6 Fiction  (4/11)
 8 Comics & Humor  (1/1)
 9 Stage & Screen  (3/5)
11 Poetry & Lyrics  (3/7)
12 Non-fiction/tech  (1/3)
13 Art of Writing  (3/6)
16 Writers' Tools  (2/2)
Enter choice(s) or ALL !
```

Fig. 4.21 *Selecting a thread from a forum's Sections Menu.*

This menu varies from forum to forum, depending on the available sections, their titles, and the number of messages. The menu does give clues to the popularity of the sections. Consider section 1, General/Help, in figure 4.21, for example. Two numbers follow the section name. The first number indicates the number of subject headings in the section; essentially, 10 different conversations or threads are grouped within section 1 of the Literary Forum Sections Menu. The second number indicates the number of new messages (messages you have not yet read) in the section— in this case, 25.

To select a thread to read, you choose a section by typing the number of the section and pressing Enter. To choose a thread about fiction, for example, you pick section 6, Fiction, from the menu shown in figure 4.21. After you choose a subject from the Sections Menu, the Subjects Menu appears (see fig. 4.22).

```
The Literary Forum Subjects Menu
Subject (# msgs)
Section 6 - Fiction
 1 Really Bad Fiction  (1)
 2 Hemingway?  (1)
 3 Problem  (1)
 4 Congrats!  (8)
Enter choice(s) !
```

Fig. 4.22 *The Subjects Menu.*

You now see the four subject headings—threads—within
the specified section. The number to the right indicates the
number of messages in the thread you have not yet read.
To read the thread, type the number of the thread; for example, type 4 and press Enter to read the thread with the
subject heading *Congrats!* The first message of the thread
you have not read appears (see fig. 4.23).

```
#: 151881 S6/Fiction
    15-Jan-92  09:28:23
Sb: #151708-Congrats!
Fm: Julie Hymes 90474,2660
To: Diane Jefferson 96530,523 (X)
Did I hear something about your latest being
published? Really? Where? When? And where's
*my* autographed copy?
Julie
Oh yeah, congratulations! :)
* Reply:         151742
Press <CR> for next or type CHOICES !
```

Fig. 4.23 *The first unread message in the thread.*

Consider the parts of the message shown in figure 4.23.
The first line—#: 151881 S6/Fiction—indicates the message number and the section in which the message was

posted. The next line is the date and time the message was posted. Dates and times are translated into your local time. Regardless of the time zone in Julie's area, her message was posted at 9:28:23 A.M. your time. The time is kept in 24 hour time (13:00 is 1 P.M., 14:00 is 2 P.M., and so on; midnight is 0:00).

The third line—Sb: #151708-Congrats!—notes that the subject of this message is message #151708. In other words, this message is a reply to message number 151708, which concerns the subject Congrats!—the subject of this reply. Unless you change the subject when you reply (thereby creating a new thread), your reply takes the subject of the message to which you are replying. CIS also adds the number of the message to the subject field, as in the example.

The fourth line—Fm: Julie Hymes 90474,2660—includes the name and user ID number of the sender. In this example, the message was sent by Julie Hymes. Her user ID number follows her name.

Finally, the fifth line reveals the recipient of the message. In this case the line To: Diane Jefferson 96530,523 (X) indicates that the recipient is Diane Jefferson. Her ID number is noted to the right of her name. The X to the far right indicates that Diane has read this message.

After the body of the message, the line * Reply: 151742 appears, indicating that the message has a reply. (The number indicates the message number of the reply.)

Following a Message Thread

At the end of the message, you can press the Enter key or type **choices**. To follow the message thread, the easiest thing to do is simply press the Enter key so that the next message appears. If you want to reply to the message you have just read, however, you access the Read Action Menu, described in the following section, by typing **choices**.

Replying to a Message

To respond to a message (even messages not directed to you), you use the Read Action Menu, shown in figure 4.24. You invoke this menu by typing **choices** (or **cho**) at the `Press <CR> for next or type CHOICES !` prompt that follows the message you want to reply to.

```
The Literary Forum Read Action Menu
  1 REPLY with same subject
  2 COMPOSE with new subject
  3 REREAD this message
  4 NEXT reply
  5 NEXT SUBJECT
  6 READ reply
  7 DELETE this message
  8 Subject menu
  9 Section menu
Enter choice !
```

Fig. 4.24 The Read Action Menu.

Choose option 1, REPLY with same subject, to reply to the message you just read. CompuServe prompts you to enter your reply. Type each line, pressing Enter at the end of each line. Lines should be 138 characters or less (usually pressing Enter when the text reaches the right side of your screen is easiest). When you finish the message, type **/exit** on a blank line. The Post Action Menu appears (see fig. 4.25).

```
The Literary Forum Post Action Menu
  1 POST message on board
  2 EDIT message
  3 TYPE message
  4 MAIL via CompuServe Mail
  5 CANCEL message compose
Enter choice !1
```

Fig. 4.25 The Post Action Menu.

The Post Action Menu options are explained in the following list:

- *1 POST message on board.* Use this option to post the message you have just written.

- *2 EDIT message.* Use this option to edit the message.

- *3 TYPE message.* Use this option to type the entire message to your screen.

- *4 MAIL via CompuServe Mail.* Use this option to send the message by CompuServe Mail rather than posting it on the board (usually used for private replies).

- *5 CANCEL message compose.* Use this option to cancel composing the message. You choose CANCEL, for example, when you change your mind about sending the message.

Composing a New Message

The Forum Messages Menu option 4, COMPOSE a message, and the Read Action Menu option 2, COMPOSE with a new subject, enable you to post new messages on the board and start a new thread. When you choose either of these options, CompuServe prompts you to enter your message in the same manner that you enter messages when you create a reply. The main difference does not become apparent until you post the message (option 1 of the Post Action Menu). When you post a message, you must indicate the recipient of the message, the subject, and the section. Figure 4.26 shows the prompts that appear when you post a new message in the Issues forum.

CompuServe asks you for the name only or the name and user ID number of the recipient. Although the recipient's name is usually acceptable, posting a message to the user ID number ensures that the correct user receives the message. With this in mind, you may want to maintain a list of the user IDs of those with whom you correspond frequently.

```
Enter choice !11
To: All
Subj: Conference?
Section: 11
Is this correct (Y or N)? y
Message # 224064 posted
Press <CR> !
```

Fig. 4.26 Prompts that appear when you post a new message.

You also may post to *all* users, as shown in figure 4.26. By posting to all, any user looking for new messages in the section can see your message. Posting to all is good for general comments, invitations, and so forth. To send a message to the SYSOP, type **sysop** at this prompt; to send a private message to the SYSOP, type ***sysop**.

At this point, you can edit the message. For information and instructions on editing your message, see the earlier section, "Editing Messages."

Deleting a Message

You can delete only messages that you posted or that are directed to you. You cannot delete messages that belong to other users. Deleting a message can cause a problem, however. As implied by the name, threads are strings of messages, one connected to the other. If you delete a message, you cut the thread, making the discussion difficult for others to follow.

Normally, you only delete a posted message that requires replacement because of major misspellings or grammatical errors. To free up space on the message board, some forums with high volumes of messages ask that you delete short messages—such as "Thanks for the information!" or "Good to hear from you!"—that you have read.

When you follow a thread, you see the Read Action Menu (refer to fig. 4.24). Although shown in figure 4.24, option 7,

DELETE this message, does not appear at all times. This option appears only when you can delete the message you have just read. If, for example, you just received and read a short reply and want to help keep the message board clear, choose option 7 to delete the message. *Note:* As stated earlier, deleting a message can break a thread. Whether you should regularly delete short messages depends on the policies of the SYSOP of the forum.

If you are not following a thread and reading messages, you can delete your own messages by following these steps:

1. From the Forum Menu, choose option 2, MESSAGES.

   The Messages Menu appears (see fig. 4.27).

```
The Issues Forum Messages Menu
Message age selection = [New]
  1 SELECT (Read by section and subject)
  2 READ or search messages
  3 CHANGE age selection
  4 COMPOSE a message
  5 UPLOAD a message
Enter choice !
```

Fig. 4.27 *The Messages Menu.*

If you just posted the message, it is considered a *new* message; you can skip steps 2 and 3 and proceed to step 4.

2. Choose option 3, CHANGE age selection.

   The Change Menu appears (see fig. 4.28).

```
The Issues Forum Change Menu
 1 [*] NEW messages
 2 [ ] ALL messages
 3 [ ] STARTING message number
 4 [ ] Number of DAYS
Enter choice !4
# of days: 1
```

Fig. 4.28 The Change Menu.

3. Choose option 4, Number of DAYS.

   Type a number equal to the number of days previous
   that you posted the message. Consider today to be
   the first day (enter 1), yesterday the second day
   (enter 2), and so on.

   CompuServe returns you to the Messages Menu. The
   age selection represents the information you entered
   in step 3 (see fig. 4.29).

```
The Issues Forum Messages Menu
Message age selection = [Within 1 day]
 1 SELECT (Read by section and subject)
 2 READ or search messages
 3 CHANGE age selection
 4 COMPOSE a message
 5 UPLOAD a message
Enter choice !
```

Fig. 4.29 The Messages Menu reflecting the specified age selection.

4. From the Messages Menu, choose option 2, READ or
   search messages.

   The Read Menu appears (see fig 4.30).

```
The Issues Forum Read Menu
Read
  1 [Within 1 DAY]
  2 Message NUMBER
  3 WAITING messages for you (0)
Search [within 1 day]
  4 FROM (Sender)
  5 SUBJECT
  6 TO (Recipient)
Enter choice !
```

Fig. 4.30 *The Read Menu.*

5. Choose option 4, FROM (Sender), to find messages that you posted.

   CompuServe prompts you for the name or user ID number of the sender.

6. Enter *your* user ID number or name (or both) because you are looking for messages you sent.

   If your last name is unique, you can use only your last name to locate your message. If your last name is common (Smith or Jones, for example), you must enter your full name or user ID number. In any case, using your user ID number ensures that you locate your own messages.

   CompuServe displays the first message located. After the message, the Enter Choice! prompt appears.

7. To delete the displayed message, type **choices** (or **cho**). If this is not the message you want to delete, press Enter to read the next message you posted. When you find the correct message, type **choices**.

   The Read Action Menu appears (refer to fig. 4.24).

8. Choose option 7, DELETE this message; CompuServe deletes the message.

Searching for Messages

You have seen one example of searching for messages in the preceding section. Other options for searching out messages exist, however. Two options in the Messages Menu concern searching for messages (refer to fig. 4.29). These are options 2, READ or search messages, and 3, CHANGE age selection. The READ command displays messages based on the criteria you set with the CHANGE command.

Option 3, CHANGE age selection, concerns the age of the messages you want to search through. Normally, CompuServe assumes you want to consider only those messages you have not read before; therefore, you see the message age selection initially set to New. You can change this through the Change Menu, shown in figure 4.31, which appears when you choose option 3.

```
The Issues Forum Change Menu
  1 [*] NEW messages
  2 [ ] ALL messages
  3 [ ] STARTING message number
  4 [ ] Number of DAYS

  Enter choice !
```

Fig. 4.31 The Change Menu.

The Change Menu contains the following options:

■ *1 NEW messages.* This option searches only for messages not previously read.

■ *2 ALL messages.* This option searches through all messages on the board, regardless of age.

■ *3 STARTING message number.* This option prompts you to enter a message number that is to be the lowest number considered in the search.

■ *4 Number of DAYS.* This option prompts you for an age, in days, of messages you want to include in your search.

Option 4, Number of DAYS, expects the current day to be considered one day. To search messages posted today, for example, enter 1; to include messages posted yesterday, enter 2; and so on.

After setting the age criteria for your search, press Enter to redisplay the Message Menu; then choose option 2, READ or search messages, to specify more about the messages you are looking for. The Read Menu reappears (see fig. 4.32).

```
The Issues Forum Read Menu
Read
 1 [NEW] messages
 2 Message NUMBER
 3 WAITING messages for you (0)
Search [new] messages
 4 FROM (Sender)
 5 SUBJECT
 6 TO (Recipient)
Enter choice !
```

Fig. 4.32 The Read Menu.

This menu contains the following options:

■ *1 [NEW] messages.* This option enables you to read all messages posted since your last logon.

■ *2 Message NUMBER.* This option prompts you for the number of a message you want to read.

■ *3 WAITING messages for you.* This option enables you to read all messages posted to you. The number to the right indicates the number of messages that you have not read.

■ *4 FROM (Sender).* This option prompts you to enter a
name or user ID number; then CompuServe displays
the messages sent by the specified individual.

■ *5 SUBJECT.* This option enables you to read messages
on a specific subject; CompuServe prompts you for
the subject.

■ *6 TO (Recipient).* The option prompts you to enter a
name or user ID number; then CompuServe displays
the messages addressed to that individual.

Options 1, 4, 5, and 6 are affected by the age setting you
choose with option 3, CHANGE age selection, of the Messages Menu. Option 1, [NEW] Messages, changes according
to the setting, displaying the number of days in age you
specified. The other three options are limited to the number of days in age that you specify. If you set the age in days
to 7 (one week's time), for example, option 1 would read
[Within 7 days], and options 4, 5, and 6 would search
only messages posted within the last seven days. Options 2
and 3 are not affected by the age setting.

Using READ Commands

The menus simplify things for the new user but can slow
the more proficient user. After using the same options repeatedly, you may find yourself wondering if a faster way
than using the menus to enter the commands exists. Rather
than choosing options from menus, you can type commands to accomplish the same thing; in many cases, these
commands will fit on a single line.

To read all the messages posted to Joe Dobransky in the
past 7 days, for example, you could enter the following
command at the Messages Menu:

READ DAYS:7 TO:Dobransky

Using commands saves the several steps that are required
to use the menus. The general format for the READ command is listed in the following:

READ	[Direction]	[Age]	[Criteria:]	[Sections:]
	FORWARD	NEW	FROM:*user*	SEC:#
	THREAD	DAYS:##	TO:*user*	
	REVERSE	ALL	SUBJECT:*sub*	
	WAITING	STA:##		
	MARKED			
	NUMBER			

You can "mix 'n match" the options in this list by choosing one option from each column, as needed. The only restriction is that the age and criteria options cannot be used with REVERSE, WAITING, NUMBER, or MARKED direction option. To read a thread in section 10 with the subject *New Macintoshes*, for example, you enter the following:

    REA THR SUB:New Macintoshes

To read all messages posted to you this month, type this:

    REA DAY:30 TO:My Name 90000,123

Although shown in uppercase, you can enter the command and options in upper- or lowercase letters. You also can abbreviate the command and options to their first three letters. The options in the preceding list are explained in table 4.3:

Table 4.3 READ Command Options

Option	Function
Direction Options:	
FORWARD	Read forward in numerical order (by message number)
THREAD	Read by following thread
REVERSE	Read backward in numerical order (by message number)
WAITING	Read messages waiting for you
MARKED	Read messages you have marked
NUMBER	Read an individual message indicated by number

Option	Function
Age options:	
NEW	Read messages that were added since your last logon
DAYS:##	Read messages posted within the specified number of days (## is the number of days)
ALL	Read all messages on the board (not recommended with the number of messages on most forums)
STA:##	Read messages, starting with the specified message (## is the message number)
Criteria options:	
FROM:*user*	Read messages posted by user (*user* is the name or ID number)
TO:*user*	Read messages posted to user (*user* is the name or ID number)
SUB:*sub*	Read messages posted with subject (*sub* is the subject heading)
Sections option	
SEC:*section#*	Read messages in the specified section number (you can have more than one section number in this option by separating the numbers with commas—for example, SEC:1,3,10).

Using the Library Area

The library, which is another part of a forum's structure, is one reason why CompuServe is so popular. The library can contain anything from files submitted by users and software written by users to records of interesting discussions.

You can *download* the files in the library, transferring them to your computer. In addition, many companies provide software upgrades that registered users can download from the library, saving time in the upgrade process. Even Apple places the newest system software in a library, making it widely available to CIS users.

Defining Libraries

CompuServe libraries correspond roughly to their off-line counterpart. These libraries serve as storage areas for documents and other files. You can browse through a library and copy items to your computer.

The library area is divided into the same sections that the message board is divided into. Files related to the forum section topic are stored in the corresponding library section. In the Issues forum, for example, section 11 in the message board is Native Americans. The corresponding section 11 in the library contains files relating to the topic Native Americans.

Choosing a Library

From any Forum Menu, you choose option 3, LIBRARIES, to enter the library area. The Libraries Menu, which lists each of the library's sections, appears (see fig. 4.33).

To choose a library, type the number of the section and press Enter. You then see the menu that enables you to access the files within libraries, as shown in figure 4.34. This menu is typical of all libraries, despite the menu title.

As in a regular library, you may browse through the files by choosing option 1, BROWSE Files. When you choose this option, CompuServe prompts you to specify the library to browse. At this prompt, you press the Enter key to browse the currently selected library (as in the example below) or enter the numbers, separated by commas, of the libraries you want to browse. You also can enter *all* to browse all libraries in the forum. (Previously, you could browse only one library at a time; now you can browse more than one library, which is why you find yourself repeating your library selection.)

```
The Issues Forum Libraries Menu
 1 Around the World
 2 Political Issues
 3 Individual Liberty
 4 New Democrats
 5 Between the Sexes
 6 Parenting Issues
 7 Defense-War & Peace
 8 Selfhelp & Handicap
 9 Rush H. Limbaugh
10 Paranormal Issues
11 Native Americans
12 Men's Issues
13 General Issues
14 Seniors
15 Ethics/Human Rights
16 Adoption Today
17 Lesbian/Gay Issues
Enter choice !
```

Fig. 4.33 The Libraries Menu.

```
The Issues Forum Library 11
Native Americans
 1 BROWSE Files
 2 DIRECTORY of Files
 3 UPLOAD a File (FREE)
 4 DOWNLOAD a file to your Computer
 5 LIBRARIES
Enter choice !
```

Fig. 4.34 The menu you use to access files within libraries.

Remember that time equals money. The more time you spend browsing, the more money you spend. Some libraries are enormous and take quite a while to browse. Listing the libraries in a forum and then browsing selectively is more economical.

After entering the library (or libraries) to browse, CompuServe asks you for the *keywords*, which are single words related to the topic for which you want to locate files. In the case of the Native Americans library, for example, you may want to search for Seneca or Comanche. You can enter more than one keyword by separating the keywords with a comma or a space. You also can press Enter to browse all the files in the library; however, because some libraries are quite large, browsing all the files can produce quite an extensive listing. You may want to use option 2, DIRECTORY of Files, in the Library Menu instead.

Finally, CompuServe prompts you for the maximum age of the files you want to find. Enter a number in days that reflects the earliest file to be located. If you are interested only in files submitted in the past month, for example, type 30 and press Enter. To find all files matching your keywords regardless of age, press Enter without including a number entry. This process is illustrated in figure 4.35.

```
Enter libraries (e.g. 1,2,4 or ALL)
or <CR> for current library:
Enter keywords (e.g. modem)
or <CR> for all: powwow
Oldest files in days
or <CR> for all:
```

Fig. 4.35 Specifying libraries, keywords, and file age.

When you press Enter at the prompt, CompuServe displays the first file matching your conditions with a description of the file (see fig. 4.36).

```
[76703,266]
POWWOW.THD/Asc  Bytes:  26620, Count: 11,
   15-Oct-91(15-Oct-91)
   Title   : Powwows
   Keywords: POWWOW REACTIONS INDIANS
   This is a discussion of powwows from the
   message board.
Press <CR> for next or type CHOICES !
```

Fig. 4.36 *A file that matches your specifications.*

The items in figure 4.36 are explained in the following:

■ *POWWOW.THD.* This item indicates the name of the file. The extension THD indicates that the file is a text thread transferred from the message board. Many extensions are specific to software; for example, an IBM PC program in a library may have an extension of EXE or COM, or a file compacted by the program Stuffit may have the extension SIT. Further information is usually detailed in the description of the file.

■ *Asc.* This item indicates whether the file is an ASCII or text file.

■ *Bytes: 26620.* This item indicates the size of the file in bytes. If you know the speed of your communication package, this information can give you an idea how long downloading this file may take.

■ *Count: 11.* This item indicates the number of times the file has been downloaded. This information can give you an idea of the popularity of the file.

■ *15 Oct-91.* This item indicates the date the file was uploaded. The file in figure 4.36 was submitted about October 15, 1991 (*about* because uploaded files must be attended to by the SYSOP before they become generally available, which may take a day or two, depending on the SYSOP's work load).

■ *Title.* This item indicates the file's title.

■ *Keywords.* This item indicates all keywords you can
use to locate this file.

■ The final line is a description of the file's contents.

You can press Enter to display the next matching file or
type **choices** (or **cho**) to download this file. Downloading
files is explained in the section "Downloading Files."

Getting a File Directory

Browsing the library is fine if you have some idea of the
kind of file that you are looking for. A directory of all files
in the library can give you an idea of what is available. To
obtain a directory, choose option 2, DIRECTORY of Files,
from the Library Menu (refer to fig. 4.34). When you
choose option 2, CompuServe lists all the files in the library
(see fig. 4.37).

This list of files contains the following information for each
entry. To illustrate, notice the first entry of the list. The following explains the components of this entry:

■ *[70313,3323].* The user ID number of the user who
submitted the file

■ *NABOOK.TXT.* The name of the file

■ */Asc.* The file type (ASCII in this example, text)

■ *Bytes: 1668.* The size of the file in bytes

■ *Count: 9.* The number of times the file was downloaded

■ *08-Dec-91.* The date the file was submitted

Downloading Files

Downloading is a technical term for transferring. The *down*
part is an indication of the direction of the transfer. The
machine to which you are connected is viewed as being
above your own machine. To *download* is to transfer a file
from the machines of CompuServe to your own.

```
[70313,3323]
NABOOK.TXT/Asc  Bytes:    1668, Count:   9, 08-Dec-91
[71760,3461]
INDFOR.TXT/Asc  Bytes:    8113, Count:   5, 27-Nov-91
[70007,4625]
HAWAII.TXT/Asc  Bytes:    1870, Count:   4, 11-Nov-91
[76703,266]
LIB11.TTL/Asc   Bytes:     792, Count:  17, 28-Oct-91
TOMHWK.THD/Asc  Bytes:   10174, Count:   6, 17-Oct-91
SMLPOX.THD/Asc  Bytes:    2228, Count:  10, 15-Oct-91
POWWOW.THD/Asc  Bytes:   26620, Count:  11, 15-Oct-91
(15-Oct-91)
HIST.TXT/Asc    Bytes:    5867, Count:   9, 15-Oct-91
[70411,472]
BOOKS.TXT/Asc   Bytes:    1319, Count:  19, 15-Oct-91
Last:14-Jan-92
[71307,2020]
INDGEN.SMP/Asc  Bytes:   39899, Count:  14, 25-Sep-91
[70307,675]
OFFAIR.TXT/Asc  Bytes:    5999, Count:   5, 23-Aug-91
[76703,266]
AMINDS.THD/Asc  Bytes:   75564, Count:   6, 19-Jul-91
TERMS.THD/Asc   Bytes:   14347, Count:  13, 21-Apr-91
PLIGHT.THD/Asc  Bytes:   17225, Count:  13, 21-Apr-91
[76066,3721]
WRTERS.TXT/Asc  Bytes:    1117, Count:  12, 20-Apr-91
TREATY.TXT/Asc  Bytes:    2679, Count:  19, 20-Apr-91
[76703,266]
KNEE.THD/Asc    Bytes:   16977, Count:  11, 20-Apr-91
[76066,3721]
PAPERS.TXT/Asc  Bytes:    3124, Count:  44, 18-Apr-91
LPELTR.TXT/Asc  Bytes:    4996, Count:  15, 18-Apr-91
```

Fig. 4.37 A list of files contained within the specified library.

Downloading can be a bit complicated and requires some investigation on your part. If you are using a communications package other than CompuServe Information Manager, TAPCIS, or Navigator (covered later in this book), you must determine the type of transfer protocols that you have available.

A *transfer protocol* is a set of rules governing the exchange of information between two computers. By abiding by the same rules on each side, the communicating machines know what to expect from each other. Your communications package should be able to use at least one and probably several transfer protocols. Check the manual for more information.

To download a library file, you first choose option 3, LIBRARIES, from the Forum Menu; then choose the library that contains the appropriate file or files. CompuServe presents the Library Menu (refer to fig. 4.34). If you know the name of the file you want to download, use the following steps to download the file:

1. Choose option 4, DOWNLOAD a file to your Computer, from the Library Menu.

2. Enter the name of the file you want to download and press Enter.

    The Library Protocol Menu appears (see fig. 4.38).

```
Library Protocol Menu
Transfer protocols available -
 1 XMODEM
 2 CompuServe B+ and original B
 3 DC2/DC4 (Capture)
 4 YMODEM
 5 CompuServe QB (B w/send ahead)
 6 Kermit
 0 Abort transfer request
Enter choice !
```

Fig. 4.38 The Library Protocol Menu.

3. Type the number of the protocol your communications package can use and press Enter.

4. Enter a name under which the file should be stored on your computer and press Enter.

   CIS begins the transfer.

5. Choose the command in your communications package that enables it to receive the file transfer.

   When the transfer is finished, press Enter to continue using CIS.

Some protocols are more efficient at transferring data than others. In general, you should use the most efficient protocol available to quicken the download and save money. The following list shows protocols ranked from fastest to slowest:

1. Z MODEM (usually not available on CIS)
2. Y MODEM
3. CompuServe QB
4. CompuServe B
5. X MODEM
6. DC2/DC4
7. Kermit

If you are browsing files (option 1 in the Library Menu), you can download a file you have just seen described by typing **choices** (or **cho**) at the prompt, as shown in figure 4.39.

```
[76703,266]      Lib:11
AMINDS.THD/Asc  Bytes:   75564, Count:
   6, 19-Jul-91
   Title   : American Indians/Iraqis
   Keywords: NATIVE AMERICANS INDIANS IRAQIS
    PARALLEL
   Some people see a parallel between the
    American Indians and the
   Iraqis. In this file users discuss this
    topic.
Press <CR> for next or type CHOICES !cho

The Issues Forum Library Disposition
 1 READ this file
 2 DOWNLOAD this file
 3 DESCRIPTION
 4 RETURN to library menu
Enter choice or <CR> for next !2
```

Fig. 4.39 Downloading file after you read a file's description.

Choosing option 2, DOWNLOAD this file, from the Library Disposition Menu is the same as step 1 in the preceding steps. You then follow the remaining steps to complete the download.

Before downloading, you can get more information on the file by choosing option 3, DESCRIPTION. If the file is text (indicated by the /Asc notation in figure 4.39), you can read the file on-line by using option 1, READ this file.

Reading a file on-line is not recommended because it takes time, for which you are charged. Downloading the file and then reading it when you are not logged on is faster and more economical.

If your communication program does not have Y Modem or CompuServe B or QB protocols, you may be able to install these protocols. Check your program's documentation to see if you can install external protocols. If so, you can download the protocol from CIS and install it on your communication program. Installing one of these protocols makes your downloads go more quickly, meaning you spend less money.

Uploading a File

Uploading is the reverse of downloading: you transfer a file *from* your computer *to* the library. To encourage you to submit files, CompuServe suspends connect charges while you upload a file so that you incur only network charges (and long distance charges if you are calling a node outside your local area) while uploading.

Uploading is done for various reasons. You can upload a software program that you wrote and want to share with others, for example, or you can submit a story in the Literary forum or a list of reference books concerning a political issue in the Issues forum. In any case, certain rules pertain to uploading files. By uploading, you are implicitly stating to CIS that you have the right to publish the material. This means that you hold the copyright or have permission to distribute the information; consequently, you are liable for copyright infringements. If you are uncertain about uploading a file, ask the SYSOP first.

All uploaded files are checked by the SYSOPs before being placed in the library; therefore, a file you upload does not immediately become available. The SYSOPs check the material for potential copyright problems, virus infection, and so forth. Your user ID number accompanies the upload; there is no such thing as an "anonymous" upload.

To begin an upload, enter the library area by choosing option 3, LIBRARIES, from the Forum Menu; then choose the

library you want to submit to. When the Library Menu
appears, choose option 3, UPLOAD a File; CompuServe
prompts you for the name of the file. This is the name that
appears in the library, not the name of the file on your
disk. You are limited to six characters, a period, and a three
letter extension (see fig. 4.40).

```
The Issues Forum Library 11
Native Americans
 1 BROWSE Files
 2 DIRECTORY of Files
 3 UPLOAD a File (FREE)
 4 DOWNLOAD a file to your Computer
 5 LIBRARIES
Enter choice !3
Suspending connect charges...
Under our Agreement and Operating Rules,
you must own or have sufficient rights to
any information you place on the Service.
File name: NABOOK.TXT
```

Fig. 4.40 *Information required to upload a file.*

After you enter the file name, the Library Protocol Menu,
shown in figure 4.41, appears. Choose the protocol that
your communications package uses for file transfers.

```
Library Protocol Menu
Transfer protocols available -
 1 XMODEM
 2 CompuServe B+ and original B
 3 DC2/DC4 (Capture)
 4 YMODEM
 5 CompuServe QB (B w/send ahead)
 6 Kermit
 0 Abort transfer request
Enter choice !1
```

Fig. 4.41 *The Library Protocol Menu.*

After you choose a protocol, CompuServe asks for the transfer type (see fig. 4.42). Choose a transfer type that fits your file.

```
Transfer types available -
1 ASCII
2 Binary
3 Image
4 Graphic:RLE
5 Graphic:NAPLPS
6 Graphic:GIF
Enter choice !1
Starting XMODEM receive.
Please initiate XMODEM send
and press <CR> when the transfer
is complete.
```

Fig. 4.42 *Available transfer types.*

The available transfer types are explained in the following list:

- *1 ASCII.* Special text files that contain no special formatting codes. Check your word processor's manual to determine how to save files as ASCII text (also called ASCII or text).

- *2 Binary.* Machine language programs (software) and other binary information, for example, BIN files on the IBM PC.

- *3 Image.* Binary files specific to a particular machine, for example, IMG files on the IBM PC.

- *4 Graphics:RLE.* Run-Length Encoded graphics.

- *5 Graphics:NAPLPS.* North American Presentation Level Protocol Syntax graphics.

- *6 Graphics:GIF.* Graphics Interchange Format graphics.

Your software may or may not support the graphics types; however, conversion programs do exist and are available from CIS. Check the Graphics forum or the forum specific to your computer for more information. GIF and RLE formats are used extensively on CIS. You may want a program that converts these formats to and from the format(s) used by your software.

Choose the command in your communications package that enables the communications package to transmit the file. At the end of the transfer, press Enter to continue using CIS.

Using the Conference Area

The conference area, as the name suggests, is the electronic equivalent of the conference room. Rather than "talking," people type their words, and rather than "listening," people watch what others type. Users gather in this area to engage in informal chats or more formal round table discussions with a moderator. Many forums have regularly scheduled conferences so that users can gather to discuss topics of mutual interest. Special conferences are announced by the SYSOPs. Information about the regular and special conferences can be found in the announcements.

Defining the Conference Area

The conference area is divided into *rooms* where people meet on-line. A small forum may only have one room; larger forums, on the other hand, may have several rooms.

When you enter a conference room, you are immediately connected to the other users in that room. Everything that you type appears on their screens, just as everything they type appears on your screen. In this way, several people can "talk" together. Provisions also exist to accommodate private conversations outside the "hearing" of other members of the conference room.

Understanding Conference Conventions

Two main types of conferences—the informal chat and the moderated discussion—exist. Each type of conference has certain conventions, which are discussed in this section. Other conventions may exist specific to the forum in which the conference is held, however. These conventions are listed in the conference announcements, or you can learn them by participating in a conference.

Informal conferences have few conventions, but you should keep a couple in mind. First, everything you type appears on the screens of the other members of the conference. Your name and ID number are placed to the left of your comment.

CompuServe does not permit obscene language at any time. In a conference, special care should be exercised. Even a rather innocent joke can go awry on-line. Keep in mind that the usual clues of body language and tone of voice are not present when you are in conference. You may want to review the emoticon symbols discussed in "Understanding Forum Conventions" earlier in this chapter so that, if you make a joke, you can end it with a smile :).

 If your communications program has a *chat mode*, turn it on before beginning a conference. The chat mode divides your screen in half. The top half shows what others are "saying," while the bottom half shows what you are typing. Keeping things separate can save you a great deal of time and frustration and make the conference easier and more enjoyable.

The first time you conference, you may notice that, because several users are typing simultaneously, the comments come fast and furious. In this situation, you must indicate to whom your comment is directed. You can do this by preceding your comment with the name of the person. The way of doing this varies from user to user, but the most common methods are illustrated in the following:

Judy:You said you had a degree in ethnobotany? Is that right?

Bob>Saw your message on the board. You sure about the upgrade?

Jim-When did you read that article?

To help reduce the traffic in a conference, you should make your comments short. If you do need to make a longer comment, break it up. You indicate a broken comment with ellipses (see fig. 4.43).

```
Judy-When I read your message on the board
   yesterday...
Judy-I was rather surprised. Are you saying
   that...
Judy-violets were used by Indians to heal
   people?
```

Fig. 4.43 *A message broken over several lines.*

The ellipses in figure 4.34 alert Judy that the comment is not finished and that more is coming. The question mark (or period or exclamation mark) indicates that you are finished and she may reply.

Breaking a comment is necessary not only because of the amount of typing going on in conferences but also because you are limited to a single line for each comment (about 80 characters, the usual screen width). Longer comments must be broken up.

Formal conferences have similar conventions; however, because they permit only one person at a time to speak, the problem of indicating to whom your comment is directed is less significant. Emoticons and abbreviations are used much less (if at all) because of the more formal tone of the conference. Also, because only one person at a time can type, the need to shorten comments is less urgent.

The most important formal conference convention is not to speak out of turn. A formal conference has a moderator who acts as a "traffic cop" to recognize and grant permission to speak. The moderator indicates how you request the floor to make a comment or ask a question. A common method of requesting the floor is to type a question mark (?). The moderator then chooses a person and grants permission to speak.

Joining a Conference

When you enter a forum, the number to the right of option 4, CONFERENCING, indicates whether a conference is taking place. This number shows how many people (although they may not be in the same room) are participating in conferences. To join a conference, choose option 4 from the Forum Menu. The conference announcement appears, and a menu of the conference rooms is displayed. You must choose a room to enter by typing the number of the room and pressing Enter. The comments of conference members should begin to appear on-screen.

If you join an informal conference, you should announce yourself. You can do this by typing a general hello, such as "Evening, everyone," and pressing Enter.

Shortening your name when in conference is best (and required in some forums). Shortened names reduce the screen clutter for other users. In a truly informal conference, you may want to use a short nickname. (Shorten your name before you type your hello message.)

To change your name (shorten it to initials or a first name only, for example) after entering a conference room, type **/name** *newname* and press Enter. *Newname* is the name you want to go by during the conference. Use something short: a first name (first name and initial if your first name is common) or a nickname.

In a formal conference, neither the hello message nor the name change apply. When you enter a formal conference, you should make *no* comment until the moderator outlines the rules for making comments or asking questions. If you join the conference late, watch other users to determine the proper method of requesting the floor.

Using Conference Commands

Because everything you type in conference appears on the screens of other users, commands must be done in a special way. You must precede each command with a slash (/) and enter it as the first item on a new line; for example, you cannot type *Hello everyone /Name Jim*. The hello and the command must be on separate lines.

The /USERS command, for example, enables you to get a list of the users who are participating in the current conference. If you type a room number after the command, CompuServe lists only users in that room. Type **forum** after the /USERS command to list users in the forum but not in conference. Type **all** after the command to list all users in the forum. The /USERS command displays a listing similar to the one shown in figure 4.44.

```
User   User ID     Node   Rm   Name/Forum Area
  10   70411,472   LKC    11   Mark
  13   90566,000   NYK    11   Joe
  17   88888,123   NNM    11   Judy
```

Fig. 4.44 Listing users participating in a specified conference.

The number under User is the user number (or job number), different from the user ID number. Many of the conferencing commands, listed in table 4.4, require the user number.

Table 4.4 Conference Commands

Command	Result
/BREAK	Exit a private conversation and rejoin the conference room
/DAY	Display the current date and time
/ECHO	Turn screen echo on
/EXIT	Leave the conference room and return to the forum
/INVITE *x*	Send an invitation for a private conversation to a member of the conference; *x* is the user number (not user ID number); see the information regarding the /USERS command that precedes the table
/JOB	Display your user number
/JOIN	Accept the invitation to a private conversation; only works after you receive an invitation
/MONIT *x*	Monitor the conversation in one or two other rooms without leaving the room you are in; *x* is the room to be monitored; add a second room by adding a comma and the other room number
/NAME *newname*	Change your name to *newname*
/NOECHO	Turn off screen echo; use only if you are an expert typist because, although you cannot see your comments until you press Enter, all conference participants see them
/NOINVITE	Block invitations to private conversations from other users
/NOPAGE	Block paging by other members; to later enable paging, type /**page**
/NOSEND	Block messages sent with /SEND; type /**send** to later enable messages to you

continues

Table 4.4 Continued

Command	Result
/NOUID	Cancel the UID command, that is, stop including user numbers with messages
/PAGE x	Page another user in the conference area; x is the user number or user ID number
/ROOM x	Switch to another conference room; x is the new room number
/SEND x message	Send a 73 character maximum private message to a user; x is the user number; *message* is the message text
/SQUELCH name /SQUELCH x /SQUELCH uid	Block out the comments of the named person, the user number (x), or the user ID (*uid*)
/STATUS	Display the numbers of users in each conference room
/UID	Add the user number to the conference message of other users (user numbers are not the same as user ID numbers; see information about the /USERS command that precedes the table)
/UNMON x	Disable monitoring of room x
/USERS	List users participating in the current conference
/WHO	Display information (including user number) about the last person who commented in the conference; specify a user number or a user ID number after the command to get information on another person

Using Forum Options

The OPTIONS command of the Forum Menu enables you
to set various options that affect how the forum displays
messages. After you choose option 7, the FORUM OPTIONS
menu appears (see fig. 4.45).

```
FORUM OPTIONS
  1 INITIAL menu/prompt            [Forum]
  2 Forum MODE                     [MENU]
MESSAGES OPTIONS
  3 PAUSE after messages           [Always]
  4 NAME                   [Mark K. Bilbo]
  5 Prompt CHARACTER                    []
  6 EDITOR                      [LINEDIT]
  7 SECTIONS                       [...]
  8 HIGH msg read               [224431]
  9 REPLIES info                 [Count]
 10 TYPE waiting msgs               [NO]
 11 SKIP msgs you posted            [NO]
LIBRARY OPTIONS
 12 Library DISPLAY               [Long]
```

Fig. 4.45 The FORUM OPTIONS menu.

The options of the FORUM OPTIONS menu are explained
in the following:

■ *1 INITIAL menu/prompt.* This option enables you to
choose whether you see the Forum Menu, Messages
Menu, Libraries Menu, or Conferences Menu upon
entering the forum. You should leave this option set
to Forum Menu.

■ *2 Forum MODE.* This option enables you to turn off
the menus you normally see and have only a command prompt. Leave this set to MENU until you become so proficient at CIS commands that the menus
are a nuisance.

■ *3 PAUSE after messages.* You may choose Never, Always, or To You so that CIS doesn't pause after displaying a message (Never), always pauses after displaying a message (Always), or pauses only after displaying a message addressed to you (To You). This option, discussed in the next section, can save time on CIS.

■ *4 NAME.* This option enables you to change your name on the forum.

■ *5 Prompt CHARACTER.* This option, which enables you to set a prompt character, is usually only used with script files that need a character to indicate when the next command can be sent.

■ *6 EDITOR.* This option enables you to choose between the two editors offered by CompuServe. LINEDIT provides line numbers and is the easiest to use. EDIT does not provide line numbers but is preferred by many users.

■ *7 SECTIONS.* This option permits you to enable or disable sections (within those you are authorized to use by the SYSOPs). By blocking out sections whose messages you are not interested in reading, you can reduce the number of messages in a READ command.

■ *8 HIGH msg read.* This option indicates the number of the highest message you have read. New messages are considered to be those with a higher number than this. This number is automatically updated, but you may reset it to a lower number, which enables you to "back up" and get messages you may have missed.

■ *9 REPLIES info.* At the end of a message, CIS specifies the reply information. You can set the reply information to NONE (no reply information), LIST (display the message numbers of the replies), or COUNT (indicate the number of replies).

■ *10 TYPE waiting msgs.* Set this option to YES to display automatically all new messages to you when you enter the forum; set to NO if you want replies to wait until you issue a READ command.

■ *11 SKIP msgs you posted.* Set this option to YES to ignore your own messages in READ commands; set to NO to include your messages along with others.

■ *12 Library DISPLAY.* This option specifies whether library displays will be long and informative or brief.

After you have set the options you desire, pressing Enter causes CompuServe to display the prompt shown in figure 4.46.

```
Would you like current settings
to apply to this Session only,
or to be Permanent?
Enter S or P, or H for help:
```

Fig. 4.46 Indicating whether the changes should be permanent.

Type **S** if you want the changes to apply only until you log off. Type **P** if you want the changes to apply until you next change them. Type **H** to acquire further help.

After pressing Enter, you again see the Forum Menu.

Saving Money on Forum Use

After a while, you may notice that your forum use increases. In general, when you find a forum you like, you make greater use of it. Unfortunately, your bill increases as well.

 One of the ways you can save money with CIS is to purchase one of the automated programs such as Navigator for the Macintosh, TAPCIS for the IBM, or the Information Manager for either machine. These programs automate many tasks, enabling you to read and create messages, for example, without being connected to CIS.

If you are unable to use one of these programs or do not want to purchase them, you still can save money. The first way to save money is to change option 3, PAUSE after messages, of the FORUM OPTIONS menu to NEVER. You can turn on your communications package's capture buffer and save your messages as files (check your manual for information on doing this).

After turning the buffer on, enter the message area and issue the appropriate READ command, such as READ NEW to read all new messages or READ WAITING to read messages waiting for you. The messages scroll by at the maximum speed of your modem. You probably will not be able to read the messages as they scroll by; however, this is not important as long as your communications package stores the messages on disk so that you can read them later.

When you have gone through all your messages, turn your capture buffer off and log off of CIS immediately. When you are off-line, use your word processor or any ASCII text reader to open the file you just created for your messages.

The reverse can be done to answer messages; however, this procedure is a bit more complicated. The idea is to duplicate your actions, commands, and so forth in a text file and then transmit that text file to CIS. By transferring a text file that contains your actions and commands, you can reply to messages almost as quickly as your modem can transmit.

Set option 2, Forum MODE, in the FORUM OPTIONS menu (refer to fig. 4.45) to PROMPT rather than MENU for the following. For example, suppose that you receive a message with a header, as shown in figure 4.47, that you want to post a reply to.

```
#: 152354 S9/Stage & Screen
   17-Jan-92  21:03:47
Sb: #152347-Opera
Fm: D. Lynn Smith 90023,123
To: B. Smart 90505,456
```

Fig. 4.47 A message containing a header.

The top number, 152354, is the number of the message.
To record your message before you send it, you type the
following in a text file created with a word processor
(you aren't logged on at this point):

REPLY

152354

Personally I rather liked Phantom. I don't know what

everyone is complaining about.

Bob

/EXIT

POST

Each line must end in a carriage return; do _not_ rely on
your word processor's word wrap. Make certain that you
save the file as text.

You can then enter CompuServe's message area and, at the
Messages! prompt, use your communications package to
upload the file as text (ASCII). Each line is sent to CIS as if
you were typing it in (though very quickly). The items of
your reply are explained in the following:

- *REPLY.* The REPLY command indicates to CIS that you
  want to reply to a message.

  152354. This item is the number of the message to
  which you want to reply.

- *Personally I rather...* This is the body of your reply.

- */EXIT.* This item is the editor command that indicates
  your message is complete.

- *POST.* This command posts the message.

You can put more than one reply in a file, but you should
not leave any blank lines in the file except in the body of a
message. There should be no blank lines before the first
REPLY command, no blank lines between commands,
and no blank lines between the POST command of one

message and the REPLY command of the next. Keep in mind that as far as CIS knows, you are typing the lines; consequently, a blank line indicates to CIS that you pressed the Enter key without typing a command first.

Note: You can have blank lines in the message text because the message text is sent to the edit program. This program (whether LINEDIT or EDIT) accepts blank lines to enable you to add space between your paragraphs. The /EXIT command indicates that the message is finished and causes the Post Action! prompt to appear.

You can even automate your log on and the GO codes for a forum in a file to further speed your message posting and save money. Such a file would resemble the one shown in figure 4.48.

```
90023,123
My*Password
Go Issues
Reply
12345
Listen, I think Bush...
Me
/Exit
Post
Reply
12456
Are you sure...
Me
/Exit
Post
Off
Off
```

Fig. 4.48 *Automating the logon and GO codes for a forum.*

For those familiar enough with communications packages, the preceding may suggest a script, and, indeed, it is very similar. You may want to experiment with creating a script to automate CIS functions.

If you are not familiar with the concept of scripts and you own a Macintosh or IBM PC (or clone), you should consider one of the autopilot programs mentioned previously. These programs handle all scripting so that you don't have to worry about learning what a computer script is.

Using CompuServe Mail

In addition to the forum message area, CompuServe offers an electronic version of mail that permits private messages between users. In addition to sharing messages with other CIS users, you can send your messages to the outside world by way of FAX, MCI Mail, Telex, and the Internet computer network. Other such "gateways" may be offered as the system expands, giving you even more options for your electronic mail.

Defining CompuServe Mail

CompuServe Mail is an electronic messaging system. You can compose a message on-line or upload a message you created earlier. Messages composed on-line are text, just like letters you mail through the post office. Uploaded messages, however, can be in text or binary format (a binary message, for example, may be a software program you want to send to someone).

CompuServe Mail is much faster than its "real world" counterpart—the U.S. Postal Service. Delivery takes place in a matter of moments or a few hours rather than days. You address the mail by using the CompuServe user ID number of the recipient or another routing code, such as a FAX number.

Reading Mail

When you log on to CompuServe, the system notifies you if you have mail with the message `You have Electronic Mail waiting`. To read the mail, type **go mail** at the exclamation mark (!) prompt. The CompuServe Mail Main Menu appears (see fig. 5.1).

```
CompuServe Mail  Main Menu
  1 READ mail, 1 message pending
  2 COMPOSE a new message
  3 UPLOAD a message
  4 USE a file from PER area
  5 ADDRESS Book
  6 SET options
  9 Send a CONGRESSgram ($)
```

Fig. 5.1 The CompuServe Mail Main Menu.

Option 1, READ Mail, indicates the number of messages waiting for you. In the sample menu, for example, 1 message is waiting. To read the message, choose option 1 by typing **1** and pressing Enter. The Read Menu, which enables you to choose what message to read first, appears. Type the number of the message and press Enter.

After reading the message, the Action Menu automatically appears. This menu gives you the following options:

■ *1 DELETE this message.* This option deletes the message (if you delete a message accidentally, you can restore it by typing **undelete** and choosing the message from the menu; you must do this before leaving the mail system, however, or the message is lost permanently).

- *2 FILE in PER area.* This option enables you to store the message in your personal storage area.

- *3 FORWARD.* This option enables you to forward the message to someone else. You can forward to FAX, Telex, and similar services by entering the proper routing information (covered later in this chapter).

- *4 REREAD this message.* This option enables you to reread the message.

- *5 REPLY.* This option enables you to compose a reply to the message. You are not prompted for the subject or the address because this information is taken from the message you just read.

- *6 SAVE in mailbox.* This option saves the message in your mailbox storage area. Rather than using this option, you probably are more likely to use option 7, DOWNLOAD Message, or read the message with your communication package's capture option turned on (thus storing the message on your computer).

- *7 DOWNLOAD message.* This option downloads the message to your computer.

After you read, reply to, or download a message, you still must delete or file it; otherwise, the message remains in your mailbox. Although you can use option 6, SAVE in Mailbox, to save the message in your mailbox, you are limited to 50 messages. If you reach this limit, CompuServe rejects new mail. Downloading or filing the message and then deleting it is best.

Creating and Sending Mail

Creating a message on-line is called *composing* You type the message, edit it if needed, and then send it. You also

can *upload* messages that were created in a word processor (the message must be stored in ASCII format, however)
and then send them. Keep in mind that you are limited to
50,000 characters or 1,000 lines. If your line length is 80
characters (the normal width), you can mail approximately
625 lines. Additional limits, explained in later sections, may
exist if you use the FAX, Internet, or other mail options.

Composing Mail

To send a mail message, choose option 2, COMPOSE a
New Message, from the CompuServe Mail Main Menu. A
prompt asking you to compose the message appears (see
fig. 5.2).

```
CompuServe Mail  Compose
Enter message. (/EXIT when done)
 1: Bob,
 2:
 3: I got the copy of the report you sent
    but haven't had
 4: time to read it yet. I'll get to it
    soon (promise!) and
 5: drop you a line.
 6:
 7: Joe
 8: /exit
CompuServe Mail  Send Menu
```

Fig. 5.2 Composing a message.

You compose mail messages using the same techniques
you use to compose forum messages. Type each line, pressing Enter at the end of the line. You can create blank lines
by pressing Enter. When you complete your message, you
can exit the composing mode by typing /**exit** and pressing
Enter.

Sending Mail

After you compose a message and then type /**exit** and press
Enter, the Send Menu appears (see fig. 5.3).

```
For current message
 1 SEND
 2 EDIT
 3 TYPE
 4 TYPE/POSTAL
 5 FILE DRAFT copy
 6 SEND with /RECEIPT ($)
```

Fig. 5.3 *The Send Menu.*

Choose option 1, SEND, to transmit the message.
CompuServe prompts you to provide the recipient's name,
the subject, and other information (see fig. 5.4). In the
Send To field, you must enter the recipient's CompuServe
ID number or some other electronic address, as explained
in the section "Using Other Send Options." You can enter
the user's name before the user ID number; however, this
is optional. After you respond, CompuServe displays the
information for review, as shown in figure 5.5.

```
Send to (Name or User ID): Bob Jones
92127,3210
Subject: Testing 1, 2, 3
```

Fig. 5.4 *Entering the user ID number and subject information.*

```
To:   92127,3210  Bob Jones
From: Joe Dobransky
Subj: Your report
Are your message and address correct?
(Y or N)! y
Message sent to 92127,3210
```

Fig. 5.5 Reviewing the information you just typed.

Editing Mail

The Send Menu also enables you to edit the message by choosing option 3, TYPE, or option 4, TYPE/POSTAL. Choose option 4 if you plan to send this message through the U.S. Postal Service (covered later in this chapter).

Option 3, TYPE, enables you to read and *proof* the message, that is, check for errors to determine whether editing is necessary. If you must edit the message, choose option 2, EDIT. When you choose option 2, the Edit Menu appears (see fig. 5.6).

```
CompuServe Mail Edit Menu
  1 CHANGE characters in line
  2 REPLACE line
  3 DELETE line
  4 INSERT new line(s)
  5 TYPE all lines
  6 TYPE/POSTAL all lines
  0 SEND message
```

Fig. 5.6 The CompuServe Mail Edit Menu.

The Edit Menu offers the following options:

■ *1 CHANGE characters in line.* This option enables you to change one or more letters (a word, phrase, and so forth). CompuServe prompts you for the number of the line that you want to change, displays the specified line, and prompts you to enter the characters to be changed.

■ *2 REPLACE line.* This option enables you to replace an entire line. CompuServe prompts you for the line number you want to replace and then prompts you to type the new line.

■ *3 DELETE line.* This option enables you to delete a line. CompuServe prompts you for the number of the line to be deleted.

■ *4 INSERT new line(s).* This option enables you to insert one or more new lines in the message. CompuServe prompts you for the number of the line that the new line(s) should follow. Enter 0 (zero) to insert the line(s) at the beginning of the message. CompuServe presents you with line numbers until you type /**exit** to end the insert procedure.

■ *5 TYPE all lines.* This option types the message on your screen, enabling you to read it.

■ *6 TYPE/POSTAL all lines.* This option types the message on-screen in the postal format, which is different from the usual display (see the section "Sending through the U.S. Postal Service" for more information on the postal display).

■ *0 SEND message.* This option sends the message. CompuServe prompts you for the address of the recipient and the subject of the message.

Using Other Send Options

A variety of other options are available for sending mail messages. You can request a return receipt, which informs you that the recipient received the message. You can send the message to more than one person. You also can send the message by FAX, MCI Mail, the U.S. Postal Service, Telex, or the Internet computer network.

Sending with a Receipt

To send a message and request a return receipt, choose option 5, SEND with RECEIPT, from the Send Menu. The dollar sign to the right of this option indicates that an additional fee is charged for this service (check with CompuServe for current rates). The remainder of the send procedure is the same—CompuServe prompts you for the recipient and subject.

Sending to More than One Recipient

After choosing one of the send options, CompuServe prompts you indicate the recipient. At this point, you can enter more than one user ID number. Separate the addresses with a semicolon (;), as shown in the following:

    Bob 90234,839;Julie 90239,110

You also can combine CompuServe user IDs with other addresses in this manner. You may use MCI Mail to send the message to one person and CIS Mail to send it to someone else, for example:

    MCIMAIL:234-3456;Bob 90234,839

When an address is not preceded with the name of another service, such as MCIMAIL: in the example, the address is assumed to be a CIS user id.

Sending by FAX

CompuServe Mail enables you to send to any group three FAX messages that you can *direct-dial* (no operator assistance is required). You are charged a fee for FAX messages. At the CompuServe Mail Main Menu, type **help fax prices** to find out about current rates. To send your message to a FAX machine, enter **>fax:** followed by the FAX number at the Sent To prompt:

    >FAX:14095551212

Include *1* and the area code even if you are sending a FAX message to your own country and area code. (Note that the number is not separated by the traditional phone number dividers, such as parentheses and hyphens.)

You can send messages to international FAX machines. Enter **>fax:** as before, followed by the country code, the area or city code, and then the phone number of the FAX machine.

FAX messages are limited to 50,000 characters or 1,000 lines (whichever comes first). A receipt confirming that the FAX was transmitted successfully is mailed to your user ID. CompuServe Mail attempts to send your FAX five times before giving up.

Sending to Easylink

CompuServe Mail now has a connection to AT&T Easylink. To send mail to a user on Easylink, enter the address as follows at the Send To prompt:

>x400:(C=US;A=WESTERN
UNION;S=*surname*;G=*givenname*;D=ELN:*idnumber*)

Enter the surname (last name) of the individual at the surname prompt, the first name at the givenname prompt, and the recipient's Easylink number at the idnumber prompt. The command contains no spaces between address elements.

Sending through MCI Mail

To send a message through the MCI Mail system, at the Send To prompt, enter **>mcimail:** followed by the MCI Mail number or registered name, as shown in the following examples:

MCIMAIL:123-2345

MCIMAIL:Bob B. Jones

The messages, limited to 50,000 total characters, must have no more than 80 characters per line. CompuServe charges an additional fee for using MCI Mail. Type **help mcimail** at the CompuServe Mail Main Menu to find out about current rates.

Sending through the U.S. Postal Service

To send a message to an individual who does not have an electronic connection (CIS, MCI Mail, and so on), you can use the U.S. Postal Service. To do this, you use CIS to send the letter to the post office, where it is laser printed and mailed. Such messages are limited to a total of 219 lines of 80 characters each.

To send a message by U.S. Postal Service, type **>postal** at the Send To prompt, which appears after you upload or compose a message. CompuServe then prompts you for the address.

Sending by Internet

Internet is an enormous mail system that connects various governmental institutions, schools, and commercial companies. You incur no additional charges for sending your mail through this system. (*Note:* You cannot send commercial messages; for example, you cannot advertise goods or solicit or offer jobs.)

To send a message through Internet, type **>internet:** followed by the Internet address at the Send To prompt, shown in the following example:

> >INTERNET:Jones@osbb.zeron.com

Obtain the Internet address from the person you want to mail to. Internet messages are limited to 50,000 characters.

Sending by Telex

A mail message may be sent to any Telex I or II machine. An additional fee is charged for this service (type **help telex** or **help telex international** to find out about current rates).

To send a message by Telex, enter **>tlx:** followed by the machine number and—optionally—the answerback, as in the following example:

> >TLX: 3455987 ZERON

The answerback must be correct and exact for the transmission to work. If you are uncertain of its accuracy, omit it.

You receive a mail message confirming that your Telex message was received.

Sending a Congressgram

Option 9, Send a Congressgram, of the CompuServe Mail Main Menu enables you to send a letter to a legislator, the President, or the Vice President. (An additional fee—about $1.00 per message—is charged for the service.)

After choosing this option, CompuServe prompts you for the recipient's name and title. After you provide this information, you can type the text of your message. Finally, CompuServe prompts you for the subject, your name, and your postal address.

Note that if you need help locating your representatives, you can type **go fcc-1** at any ! prompt to see a state-by-state listing.

Bypassing Send Prompts

To save some time, you can enter the address of the recipient and the subject in the message itself. If the recipient and subject are indicated in the message, CompuServe Mail doesn't prompt you for this information when you send the message (whether uploaded or composed).

Enter the information at the top of the message, as shown in figure 5.7.

```
To: Joe 90847,123
Fr: Tim
Subject: Ethnobotany thread
Have you been reading...
```

Fig. 5.7 Including the address and subject in the message.

The address and subject must be at the top of the message (within the first ten lines that are not blank). You can omit the user ID number if the recipient's name is in your address book.

Uploading and Downloading Mail

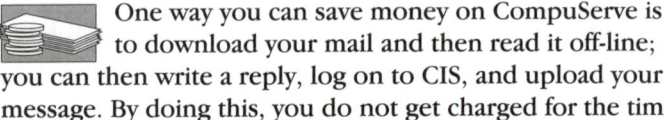 One way you can save money on CompuServe is to download your mail and then read it off-line; you can then write a reply, log on to CIS, and upload your message. By doing this, you do not get charged for the time it takes to read, compose, and edit your mail on-line.

When you are writing messages you intend to send through CompuServe Mail, you should save the message as ASCII text. Most word processors have an option that enables you to do so. If you don't know how to save a message as ASCII text, refer to your manual for information and instructions.

One exception to this rule exists: if you are sending your mail to a recipient who uses the same word processor that you use *and* you are sending the mail to a CompuServe user ID (you cannot send the message via FAX, MCI Mail, or other such options), saving the message as ASCII text is not required. If your situation meets these criteria, you can save the file in your usual word processor format and send it as a binary file that the recipient downloads (more information about binary files is provided later in this chapter).

After you enter CompuServe Mail, you can upload mail by choosing option 3, UPLOAD. The Protocol Menu appears (see fig. 5.8).

Select the protocol that is supported by your communications package (check your communications package manual to see which protocol you can use—XMODEM is perhaps the most common).

After choosing the protocol, CompuServe may ask for additional information; the Transfer Type Menu appears, for example, if you choose XMODEM (see fig. 5.9).

```
CompuServe Mail   Protocol Menu
Transfer protocols available -
  1 XMODEM (MODEM7) protocol
  2 CompuServe 'B' protocol
  3 DC2/DC4 CAPTURE protocol
  4 NO Protocol
  5 Kermit
  6 CompuServe Quick 'B' protocol
```

Fig. 5.8 *The CompuServe Mail Protocol Menu.*

5

```
CompuServe Mail   Transfer Type
  1 ASCII
  2 ColorMail
  3 Binary
```

Fig. 5.9 *The Transfer Type Menu.*

Use ASCII to send mail unless you are sending a file formatted for a particular word processor, a software program, or other nontext material for a specific word processor.

A message appears, telling you that the transfer has begun. Choose the command in your communications package that uploads the file.

After the transfer is complete, the Send Menu appears. If you upload a file, you can type or edit the message before sending it. (Of course, the idea of uploading is to avoid doing this on-line.) To send the file, choose option 1, SEND, and enter the user ID of the recipient and the subject of the mail message.

The reverse process, downloading, enables you to transfer mail from CIS to your disk so that you can read it off-line— that is, while you are not logged on to CIS. Because the transfer rate in downloading is much faster than mail can be read, you spend less time logged on and, therefore, save money.

To download mail, choose option 7, DOWNLOAD Mail, or type **download** at this menu's prompt. If more than one message is waiting, a menu of waiting messages appears. Type the number of the message to be downloaded and press Enter. Alternatively, you can type a range (such as 1-4), a list (such as 1,3,6), or a combination of a range and a list (such as 1-3,6,8) to download only a selection of messages. To download all messages, type **0** and press Enter.

After you indicate which messages you want to download, the CompuServe Mail Protocol Menu appears (refer to fig. 5.8). You must choose one of the protocols listed. The Quick B protocol (option 6) is the fastest. The B protocol (option 2) is next fastest. Kermit and XMODEM (options 5 and 1, respectively) are slower due to error checking that makes them more reliable. You should use Kermit or XMODEM if you experience frequent noise on your phone line.

NO Protocol (option 4) only works for *text transfers*, messages that consist of only numbers and letters. You cannot use this option to transfer program files and the like, for instance, that someone may have mailed you. Use option 4 if your communications package has none of the other protocols available.

At this point, a message indicating the mail message to be downloaded appears. Some protocol selections may result in further prompts. The B protocols, for example, ask for a name for the file in which the downloaded mail will be stored, as shown in figure 5.10.

```
    1 Dwight Morgan/CO Tonight
      05-May-92 15:04 EDT 70411,472 Length 15
 1 messages and 100 characters ready for
    download
 Enter a filename for your computer: Letter
 Downloading to Letter
 [Downloading rate 8 bytes per second]
```

Fig. 5.10 Additional information required if you choose a B protocol.

You need to issue the command that enables your communications package to receive a downloaded file (see your
communications package manual). At the end of the transfer, an information message appears. You are prompted
to press enter <CR> to continue. After you do so, the
CompuServe Mail Main Menu reappears, and you may
continue.

Saving and Retrieving Mail Files

You can store mail in your personal file area, which enables
you to save mail for later reading, sending, or forwarding.
To save a mail message you receive, choose option 2, FILE,
from the Read Menu. A prompt appears, asking you to provide a name for the file. Type the file name and press Enter.
Even though you save the message to a file, you still must
delete the message from your mailbox.

To retrieve a message from your personal area, choose
option 4, USE, from the CompuServe Mail Main Menu. A
prompt appears, asking you for the name of the file to be
retrieved. You then can edit or send the message just as if
you had composed it.

Receiving Mail from Other Sources

You can receive mail from most of the systems mentioned
in the section "Using Other Send Options." The important
thing to know if you want to receive mail from these other
systems is your address because, simply enough, you must
be able to inform those who want to mail messages to you.
Your CompuServe user ID makes up part of this address.

The following is a listing of your address for those systems
from which you can receive mail. The term *userid* indicates
that you should enter your CIS user ID. Some systems,
such as AT&T, require that the sender use a period (.)
instead of a comma in the user ID.

System	CIS Address
AT&T	Country=US
	ADMD = COMPUSERVE
	PRMD = CSMAIL
	DDA = ID-*userid* (**Note:** Use a period in place of the comma in the *userid.*)
Internet	*userid*@COMPUSERVE.COM (**Note**: Use a period instead of the comma in the *userid.*)
Telex	TO: *userid*
	RE: *optional subject heading*
	(**Note:** CompuServe's machine number is 3762848 and the answerback is COMPUSERVE.)

Other mail services that are connected to CompuServe may be able to send you mail. Have the people with whom you want to correspond check with their organizations. They must at least use your user ID number to address mail to you.

Using the Address Book

If you correspond often with others in CompuServe Mail, you may find storing their addresses in your on-line address book convenient. If you store the addresses in this way, you may enter only the recipient's name (or some other name) instead of the full address at the Send To prompt.

Choose option 5, ADDRESS, from the CompuServe Mail Main Menu to access the address book. The Address Book Menu, which offers the following options, appears:

■ *1 INSERT an entry.* This option enables you to insert an address into your address book. CompuServe prompts you for a name under which to store the address and then asks you to provide the user ID number. Instead of a user ID number, you can enter a FAX number, Telex number, or other such address, as discussed in the earlier section, "Using Other Send

Options." For these numbers, use the format discussed in that section.

■ *2 CHANGE an entry.* This option enables you to change an existing address.

■ *3 DELETE an entry.* This option enables you to delete addresses you no longer use.

■ *4 LIST Address Book.* This option lists the contents of your address book, including the address number, which you must provide if you change or delete an address.

■ *5 Enter/Change your NAME.* This option enables you to change your name for use with CompuServe Mail (when you send a FAX, for example, this name is added automatically to the cover sheet).

At the Send To prompt that appears when you send a message, enter the name of the person as it appears in your address book. If you forget the exact name, type **/sea** followed by a name to search for. Alternatively, type **/dir** to display a listing of the entire address book.

Setting Mail Options

You can set three CompuServe Mail options: type of editor you use, the mode of operation, and the output paging. To set the options, choose option 6, SET, from the CompuServe Mail Main Menu. The Options Menu, shown in figure 5.11, appears.

```
CompuServe Mail  Options Menu
[ ] Represents Current Setting
    (yes/no options toggle)
 1 EDITOR uses line numbers [YES]
 2 MODE of operation is [MENU]
    (MENU, PROMPT, COMMAND)
 3 Output is PAGED [YES]
```

Fig. 5.11 The CompuServe Mail Options Menu.

The CompuServe Mail Options Menu offers the following options:

- *1 EDITOR uses line numbers.* Choosing this option *toggles*—switches from one setting to the other each time it is chosen—between YES (use line numbers) and NO (does not use line numbers).

  Use line numbers unless you know the commands for the EDIT editor, which does not use line numbers. You can find more information about this editor in your CompuServe manual. The editor discussed in this book—LINEDIT—uses line numbers.

- *2 MODE of operation is.* This option presents a menu from which you choose the appropriate mode of operation: MENU, which causes the normal menus to appear; PROMPT, which displays short prompts rather than full menus; and COMMAND, which displays only the ! prompt. Use COMMAND only if you know the mail commands well; use MENU until you become proficient with mail commands.

- *3 Output is PAGED.* This option enables paging of long messages. When the option is set to YES, long messages pause when the screen is full. When the option is set to NO, long messages scroll until the message is completed.

  To save money by capturing your messages to disk, set the Output is PAGED option to NO so that the pause is eliminated (check the manual of your communications package for more on how to do this). If you read your messages on-line, leave the option set to YES.

After setting the options, press Enter to display the CompuServe Mail Main Menu again. If you changed any options, CompuServe displays a message asking whether you want to save the changes for future sessions. Type **Y** and press Enter to save the options until you next change them. Type **N** and press Enter to save the options only until you log off.

Using Mail Commands

You do not have to use the menus when you use CompuServe Mail. Instead, you can type commands and bypass the menus, thus saving time.

Menu options consist of one word in capital letters. The capitalized word indicates the command that corresponds to that menu choice. Table 5.1 provides a brief listing of these commands.

Table 5.1 Commands Used Instead of Menu Choices

Command	Use To
ADDRESS	Access the address book
COMPOSE	Compose a message
DELETE	Delete a message (follow with message number)
DOWNLOAD	Download a message (follow with message number)
EDIT	Edit the current message in the workspace
FILE	File a message in your personal file area
HELP	Produce a list of all help topics from which you can choose (You also can type the name of the command after the Help command—**help compose**, for example.)
READ	Read a message (follow with message number or ALL)
RECEIVE ALL	Read messages without pausing between messages (use if you are capturing messages to disk)
SAVE	Save a message in mailbox (follow with message number)
SCAN	Scan messages, displaying a brief description of each

continues

Table 5.1 Continued

Command	Use To
SEND	Send a message in the workspace (uploaded or composed)
TYPE	Type a message in the workspace (uploaded or composed)
UNDELETE	Undelete the message just deleted
UPLOAD	Upload a message
USE	Use a file from your personal file area (follow the command with a file name)

Using Research Services

Among the most useful services offered by CompuServe are the research services. Currently, 15 different research systems, listed in the following, are offered:

Academic American Encyclopedia

Books in Print

Business Database Plus

Computer Library

Consumer Reports

Demographics & Government Information

Health Database Plus

IQuest

Magazine Database Plus

Magill's Survey of Cinema

Marquis Who's Who

Name/Address/Phone Directories

New Car Showroom

Newspaper Library

TV News/Information Transcripts

With so many possibilities, covering all these services is not possible in this book. Only two of them—the Academic American Encyclopedia and IQuest—are discussed.

The American Academic Encyclopedia (AAE) offered by Grolier is an on-line equivalent of the bound encyclopedia. IQuest is a database search system that links many of the reference systems together. IQuest searches, for example, can access the Books in Print database.

Although you pay an additional fee to use these systems, these services, if used carefully, can provide a wealth of information for the cost.

Accessing Research Systems

You can reach all systems in the preceding list by choosing option 10, Reference, from CompuServe's TOP menu or by typing **go references**. A menu listing the services appears. At the prompt, type the number of the service you want to access.

Using the Academic American Encyclopedia

To use the Academic American Encyclopedia (AAE), you first must move to the page that contains the encyclopedia's menu. From this menu, you can choose the option that accesses the encyclopedia's information.

Accessing the AAE

Choose option 2, Grolier's Encyclopedia, from the Reference Resources Menu to access the Academic American Encyclopedia. You also can go directly to this page by typing **go aae-1** at any exclamation mark (!) prompt. The encyclopedia's menu, shown in figure 6.1, appears.

```
CompuServe                  AAE-1
     The Online Edition of
   GROLIER'S ACADEMIC AMERICAN
            Encyclopedia
         Copyright @ 1992
 Grolier Electronic Publishing
 1 Introduction
 2 Users Guide
 3 Feedback
 4 Grolier's Background on the News ($)
 5 Search Encyclopedia ($)
```

Fig. 6.1 *The menu for Grolier's encyclopedia.*

The encyclopedia's menu offers the following options:

■ *1 Introduction.* This option presents introductory information about the encyclopedia.

■ *2 Users Guide.* This option lists commands and describes how to perform searches in the encyclopedia.

■ *3 Feedback.* This option enables you to comment on the encyclopedia.

■ *4 Grolier's Background on the News.* This option displays up-to-date information on current news. An additional fee is charged for this service, as noted by the dollar sign ($).

■ *5 Search Encyclopedia.* This option enables you to search the encyclopedia for topics of interest. An additional fee is charged for this service, as noted by the dollar sign ($).

Searching the AAE

To initiate a search of the AAE, choose option 5, Search Encyclopedia, from the encyclopedia's menu. A brief message about the use of the AAE appears, and you are prompted for a search term.

When the Search term: prompt appears, enter the topic of interest and press Enter. If CompuServe finds the topic, a menu listing the subject headings appears. From this menu, you can choose a heading and then read the entry for that subject, or your choice may present a menu of subtopics from which you can choose.

After reading an entry, press Enter at the ! prompt to redisplay the topic menu. You may then choose another topic or press Enter to back up another menu. (Pressing Enter at the ! prompt without typing a command moves you back one menu, thus enabling you to return to previous menus and explore other topics listed.)

You can initiate another search at any ! prompt by typing **se** followed by a space and the search term. To search for the word *Language*, for example, type **se language** and press Enter. *Note:* Because the Search term: prompt does not appear after the first time you begin a search, you must initiate new searches using the SE command.

Using singular, rather than plural, search terms is best. Instead of *Languages*, for example, use *Language*. CompuServe searches are not case sensitive; searching for *language*, for example, produces *Language*, *LANGUAGE*, and so on.

Keep in mind that a topic may be listed under a term other than the commonly used one. Instead of *Movies*, for example, try *Film* or *Motion Picture*. If your search turns up no entries, try another term with the same meaning.

A search term of only one or two characters brings up only those items that match exactly. A search term of three or more characters matches any item that begins with those letters. For example, searching for *it* matches only *it*; searching for *cat*, on the other hand, matches *cat*, *catalog*, *category*, and so on.

Limit a search term by placing a pound sign (#) after it. If you type *dog*, for example, you retrieve *dogwood* and other items that begin with those three letters. To find only an exact match of *dog*, type **dog#**.

Citing the AAE

You can cite the AAE in bibliographies. To do so, use the following notation (with the current year):

> The Academic American Encyclopedia, on-line edition, Grolier Electronic Publishing, Danbury, CT., 1991.

Because the AAE is on-line, volume and page number do not apply.

Using IQuest

6

IQuest (pronounced "I Quest") is a system that enables you to search as many as 800 databases, including several of the databases—such as Books in Print—listed in the References Menu. Although the service costs extra and can be quite expensive to use, the information it provides can often off-set the cost.

IQuest is not a system you should use merely to satisfy curiosity because "wandering" through IQuest can be quite expensive. When you need to do serious research, however, IQuest is a valuable tool that can help you quickly locate the information you need.

Accessing IQuest

To access IQuest, choose option 1, IQuest, from the References Menu or type **go iquest** at any ! prompt. The IQuest Menu appears (see fig. 6.2).

```
CompuServe              IQUEST
IQuest
  1 Introduction to IQuest
  2 Search Tips
  3 IQuest Pricing
  4 Access IQuest ($)
  5 IQuest Savings in January
```

Fig. 6.2 *The IQuest Menu.*

The IQuest menu provides the following options:

- ▪ *1 Introduction to IQuest.* This option presents an explanation of IQuest.

- ▪ *2 Search Tips.* This option offers tips on searching IQuest. You should either read the following section about these tips or choose this option before attempting an IQuest search.

- ▪ *3 IQuest Pricing.* This option explains the current pricing of IQuest. View this information before beginning your search so that you can anticipate your charges.

- ▪ *4 Access IQuest.* This option enables you to enter the IQuest system. The dollar sign ($) indicates that, by using this option, you incur additional charges.

- ▪ *5 IQuest Savings.* IQuest periodically offers discounts for searches in specific areas. Choose this option to see whether a discount is being offered.

To enter the IQuest system, choose option 4, Access IQuest, from this menu. CompuServe then presents the IQuest Main Menu (see fig. 6.3).

```
PRESS   TO SELECT            * Main Menu *
  1  IQuest-I    System helps select the
     database
  2  IQuest-II   Search a database of your
     choice
  3  SmartSCAN   Search multiple databases
  4  Instructions
  5  NEW! This Month: *Free* COMPUTER
     SmartSCANs; Database Updates

  H  for Help, C for Commands
Total charges thus far:    $0.00
-> 4
```

Fig. 6.3 The IQuest Main Menu.

With some 800 databases, IQuest offers three different ways to select the appropriate databases for your search. These options—IQuest-I, IQuest-II, and SmartSCAN—are explained in the section "Choosing Databases" later in this chapter.

Choose option 4, Instructions, to review instructions on using IQuest (you can read these instructions without incurring extra charges). Option 5, NEW!, explains the special (if any) currently offered.

As noted in the menu, you can type H for help and suggestions or C for a listing of commands. To help you keep track of your charges, all IQuest screens indicate how much you have spent.

Understanding IQuest Commands

IQuest is not actually part of CompuServe. Rather, CompuServe offers a link to the service; consequently, some IQuest commands are different from CompuServe commands. The different commands can be confusing if you are expecting the normal CIS commands to work.

IQuest menu commands enable you to do such things as back up one menu, access help, or list possible database scans. These commands, listed in table 6.1, are entered at the IQuest right arrow (->) prompt.

Table 6.1 Quest Menu Commands

Command	Result
B	Backs up one screen
DIR LIST	Lists the categories of the available databases
DIR *name*	Lists the databases within a category—*name* is the category
H	Accesses on-line help
L	Returns you to CompuServe (that is, logs off IQuest, not CompuServe)

continues

Table 6.1 Continued

Command	Result
M	Returns you to the Main Menu
SCAN LIST	Lists scan names
SCAN *name*	Enables you to access a scan—*name* is the name of the scan.
SOS	Accesses on-line human help (that is, you actually "converse" with someone who can answer your questions)

Screen commands, shown in table 6.2, enable you to affect the flow of information to your computer. The slash (/) shown in the first set of commands is required. The caret ($^\wedge$) shown in the second set indicates the Control key. To produce the caret, hold down the Control (Ctrl) key (or the Ctrl key equivalent for your communications package) and press the indicated letter. *Note:* Mac users normally use the Command key (⌘) instead of the Ctrl key; however, you should check with your communications manual to verify this.

Table 6.2 Screen Commands

Command	Result
/CRT	Displays prompts every 22 lines so that you can read the text before it scrolls off-screen
/PRINT	Scrolls text; use if you are capturing to a printer or file and want to scroll the text upward
/VIDEO	Displays prompts every 22 lines, just as /CRT, but also clears the screen between prompts
/VT100	Displays prompts and clears the screen between prompts for VT100 terminals

Command	Result
^C	Stops scrolling and returns to the IQuest prompt
^Q	Resumes scrolling
^S	Stops scrolling
^T	Scrolls text

Choosing Databases

As mentioned earlier, because of the number of databases offered by IQuest, knowing which database to choose can be difficult. IQuest offers the first three options of the Main Menu to help you choose databases (see fig. 6.4).

```
PRESS   TO SELECT              * Main Menu *
   1  IQuest-I    System helps select the
      database
   2  IQuest-II   Search a database of your
      choice
   3  SmartSCAN   Search multiple databases
   4  Instructions
   5  NEW! This Month: *Free* COMPUTER
      SmartSCANs; Database Updates

   H  for Help, C for Commands
Total charges thus far:    $0.00
->
```

Fig. 6.4 *The IQuest Main Menu.*

You use the following options to locate the needed database:

■ *1 IQuest-I.* This option enables you to choose from menus that break the databases into categories and subcategories. Use this option if you don't know what databases are available.

■ *2 IQuest-II.* This option enables you to select a specific database. Use this option if you know which database you want to search.

■ *3 SmartSCAN.* This option, which is the most cost-effective of the three, enables you to choose a category of databases to search. New users of IQuest should use this option because it automatically chooses databases based on the selected topic.

To choose a specific database by moving through the menus of categories, however, you can use option 1, IQuest-I. Alternatively, you can use the DIR LIST command at the IQuest prompt to list the categories; then to list the databases in a particular category, type **dir** followed by the category name. When you see the database you need, choose option 2 from the Main Menu to select the specific database.

Choose option 3, SmartSCAN, to search a group of databases within a category. The SmartSCAN option is explained in the following section.

Specifying Search Information

Before you choose option 3, SmartSCAN, from the Main Menu to begin your search, you need to understand how to specify the information that you are looking for. To perform an effective search, consider the following search tips:

■ Omit common words such as *of*, *the*, *for*, *at*, *by*, *to*, and so forth.

■ Keep your searches narrow. Because a search on *car* produces an enormous number of references, for example, you should use a more specific term, such as *Model-T*.

■ Use a slash (/) at the end of a word to match all entries that begin with your entry. *Horse/*, for example, matches *Horse Racing*, *Horseradish*, and so on.

■ Narrow a search by using *and* between words.

■ Broaden a search by using *or* between words.

■ Exclude items by using *not* before a word.

■ Group related words with parentheses ( ).

You can combine the slash (/), *and*, *or*, *not*, and ( ). For example, to search for horse or dog racing but exclude gambling, your entry would be *(Horse or Dog) and Racing not Gambling.* The entry *((American and Indian) or Cherokee or Iroquois) and Language* searches for topics on American Indian languages as well as for Cherokee or Iroquois language materials. The entry *Home and Computer/* searches for home computer items, including home computers, home computer services, and so forth.

The entry *Business/ and Computer/ not (IBM or Clone)* searches for items about business (businesses, businessmen, businesswomen, and so forth) and computers (computer technology, computer services, and so on) that are not related to IBM or IBM clones. In this case, you may be searching for business uses of non-IBM technology.

Plan your searches carefully. IQuest doesn't charge for the first "miss," but you are charged a nominal fee for subsequent searches that produce nothing. More important, IQuest charges full price for searches that produce information you are *not* looking for. In fact, IQuest offers no refunds for searches that produce material based on your criteria; in other words, you pay even if your search turns up unexpected and unwanted information.

With this in mind, being too specific at first and then broadening your search slowly is best. One way to slowly broaden your category, for example, is to add *or* conditions or use the slash (/). A "miss" is much cheaper than an incorrect "hit."

Scanning Databases

Choose option 3, SmartSCAN, from the Main Menu when you are ready to begin your scan. A menu of categories, similar to the one shown in figure 6.5, appears.

```
PRESS     TO SELECT
   1  Business
   2  Science & Technology
   4  Law, Patents, Tradenames
   5  Social Sciences & Education
   6  Arts, Literature, Religion
   7  People
   8  News
   9  General Reference
   H  for Help,  C for Commands
Total charges thus far:    $0.00
->
```

Fig. 6.5 A menu of categories that appears when you choose SmartSCAN.

Choose the category that most closely fits your search. If you choose option 5, Social Sciences and Education, for example, the subcategory menu shown in figure 6.6 appears.

```
   * SOCIAL SCIENCES & EDUCATION *
PRESS     TO SELECT
   1  Archeology, Anthropology
   2  Economics
   3  Education
   4  History
   5  Library & Information Science
   6  Public & International Affairs
   7  Philosophy
   8  Psychology
   9  Sociology
   H  for Help,  C for Commands
Total charges thus far:    $0.00
->
```

Fig. 6.6 A subcategory menu for Social Sciences and Education.

Next, choose the subcategory that best fits your search (or type **b** to back up to the category menu). If you choose option 1, Archeology/Anthropology, for example, the Enter an Archaeology/Anthropology Topic prompt—which is typical of prompts appearing at this point—appears (see fig. 6.7).

```
* ENTER ARCHAEOLOGY/ANTHROPOLOGY TOPIC *
SEARCH TIPS:  Omit all punctuation and
small, common words (examples: the, as, in,
on, for, an, of).
SEARCH EXAMPLES:  Hittite/ AND inscription/
                  civilization OR
                  civilisation
     (Sian OR Xian) AND excavation
Type H for more help and examples.
ENTER AN ARCHAEOLOGY/ANTHROPOLOGY TOPIC
->
```

Fig. 6.7 *The prompt from which you enter a topic.*

Enter the desired search criteria and press Enter. IQuest ignores the *case* (capitalization) of your search criteria; for example, *CAR, Car*, and *car* are considered the same word. (For information about specifying search criteria, see the preceding section, "Specifying Search Information.")

After you enter the information, IQuest prompts you to confirm that the search criteria are correct. If correct, type *Y* and press Enter. If the criteria aren't correct, type *N* and press Enter; then reenter the search criteria.

Your search may take a little time. The message Scanning, please wait appears repeatedly on-screen while the search is being performed. IQuest indicates when the search is complete and prompts you to press Enter to view the results. When you press Enter, the Scan Results Menu appears (see fig. 6.8).

```
Archaeology, Anthropology scan results for:  CHEROKEE AND LANGUAGE

PRESS    TO SEARCH                   Results   Format     Source Type

   1   *Arts & Humanities Search............1   reference   journals

   2    Books in Print.....................2   reference   books

   3    Magazine Index.....................3   reference   magazines

   4    National Newspaper Index...........3   reference   newspapers

   5    Dissertation Abstracts Online......12  abstract    dissertations

   6    Social SciSearch...................1   reference   journals

   7    Sociological Abstracts.............1   abstract    journals

        * Good choice for professional literature.

   H    Database descriptions

   M    Main Menu

 SOS    Online assistance

Total charges thus far:     $5.00

 ->
```

Fig. 6.8 *The Scan Results Menu.*

Notice that, at this point, you have incurred some additional charges; however, the search has produced the needed information, divided into columns. The Results column indicates the number of references in each category. The Format column gives you the format of the category; for example, *abstract* (a dissertation abstract) indicates that you do not see the entire dissertation, only the abstract with publication information. The Source Type column indicates the type of items contained in the databases in the category index (books for the Books in Print database, for example).

To view the references in a particular category, type the number of the category and press Enter. Keep in mind that when you do so, *you log on to another database outside the IQuest system*. Each time you choose a category, you incur a charge.

After you choose the category, a message indicating that the database is being logged on to appears. You will then see the references for the items located.

Make certain that you have your communications package capture buffer option turned on before you choose any of the categories. Because you are paying to retrieve the information, you want to make sure you store it on disk or print it out.

After you view the information references, the menu shown in figure 6.9 appears.

```
PRESS      TO SELECT
  1     Review results again
  5     Start a new search / return to scan
        results menu
  6     Leave System
Total charges thus far:    $14.00
->
```

Fig. 6.9 *The menu that appears after you view the information references.*

This menu provides the following options:

- *1 Review results again.* This option enables you to redisplay the same information without incurring additional charges.

- *5 Start a new search / return to scan results menu.* This option redisplays the Scan Results Menu.

- *6 Leave System.* This option enables you to leave IQuest and return to CompuServe.

Other options may appear, depending on the type of search you perform. You can type **h** for help if needed.

The Scan Results Menu retains the references until you perform another search or leave the system. To retrieve the other references, choose option 5 in the Scan Results Menu; then choose another database.

Shopping on CompuServe

CompuServe offers shopping services such as the Electronic Mall, Shopper's Advantage, and Softex. The *Electronic Mall* is the on-line equivalent of the familiar shopping mall. *Shopper's Advantage* is a discount club for members. *Softex* is the software catalog of CompuServe. This chapter provides information—how you join, browse, and place orders—about these services.

Shopping the Electronic Mall

The Electronic Mall offers a collection of stores and mail order houses that are open 24 hours a day so that you can visit, browse, and place orders at your convenience. While you are in the Mall, you do not accrue connect charges. Network charges, however, do apply.

Accessing the Mall

To enter the Mall, you can choose option 6, Electronic MALL/Shopping, from the TOP menu of CompuServe or type **go mall** at any exclamation mark (!) prompt.

When you enter the Mall, a message informs you of special offers, changes to the Mall, merchants added, and so forth. Following this message, the MALL menu appears (see fig. 7.1).

```
MALL(FREE)                        MALL
      THE ELECTRONIC MALL (R)
   1 Shop the Mall - Always FREE Connect
   2 Customer Service
   3 This Week's Mall News and Events
      Join the ELECTRONIC MALL ELITE Today
   4 Shoppers Advantage Club
   5 Meet The New Merchants
```

Fig. 7.1 *The MALL menu.*

The heading of the menu indicates that this service is free of connect charges (network charges still apply, however). To begin shopping, choose option 1, Shop the Mall. The SHOP THE MALL menu appears (see fig. 7.2). The options on this menu are explained in the following sections.

```
MALL (FREE)
SHOP THE MALL
Mall Directory of Merchants
   1 Shop by Department
   2 Shop by Merchant (Alphabetic Listings)
   3 Product Category Index
   4 Directory of Catalogs
```

Fig. 7.2 *The SHOP THE MALL menu.*

Shopping by Department

To search for a product or merchant by department, choose option 1, Shop by Department, from the SHOP THE MALL menu. The MALL DEPARTMENTS menu appears (see fig. 7.3). If the entire menu cannot fit on-screen, the message MORE ! appears. Press Enter to see the remaining departments.

```
MALL (FREE)
MALL DEPARTMENTS
 1 Arts/Music/Video
 2 Auto
 3 Books/Periodicals
 4 Business/Finance
 5 Clubs/Memberships
 6 Computing
 7 Gifts/Collectibles
 8 Gourmet Foods/Flowers/Trees
 9 Health/Beauty
10 Hobbies/Toys/Pets
11 The Mens Shop
12 The Womens Shop
13 Merchandise/Electronics
14 Office Supplies
15 Services
16 Sports/Leisure
17 Travel/Vacations
```

Fig. 7.3 *The MALL DEPARTMENTS menu.*

To choose the department that interests you, type the appropriate number (for example, type 3 for Books and Periodicals) and press Enter. CompuServe displays a listing of the merchants in that department, as shown in figure 7.4.

```
MALL (FREE)
  1 HOW TO USE THIS GUIDE
  2 BARNES & NOBLE  [BN]
      America's Best Source for Books
      VI/MC/AM/DI/CSH          US/CD/JP/OT
  3 COMPUTER SHOPPER  [CS]
      Save 44% and Receive Free Gift
      VI/MC/DB                 US/CD
  4 CREATE-A-BOOK  [CK]
      Deluxe, Personalized Books for Kids
      VI/MC/AM                 US/CD/JP/OT
  5 DATA BASED ADVISOR  [DB]
      Database Mgmt.-Applications Develpmnt
      VI/MC                    US/CD/JP/OT
  6 DOW JONES & CO.  [DJ]
      Business and financial periodicals
      VI/MC/AM                 US/CD
  7 HAWAII GENERAL STORE  [HI]
      Gifts from the 50th State
      VI/MC/AM                 US
MORE !
```

Fig. 7.4 A list of merchants for the specified department.

The MORE ! prompt indicates that the listing is not finished and that to see more merchants, you must press Enter. For more information about the merchant listing, see the section, "Understanding the Merchant Listing."

To enter the merchant's store, type the number to the left of the merchant (you can do this even if the merchant entry has scrolled off-screen) or type **go**, followed by the merchant's GO code (type **go bn**, for example, to enter Barnes & Noble).

A greeting followed by the merchant's menu appears when you enter a store. For information and instructions on placing an order, see "Ordering Products."

Shopping by Merchant

If you are looking for a specific merchant, you can search alphabetically by choosing option 2, Shop by Merchant, from the SHOP THE MALL menu. A menu similar to the one shown in figure 7.5 appears.

```
MALL (FREE)
Select choice containing first letter
of merchant name.
  1  A
  2  B - C
  3  D - E
  4  F - H
  5  I - M
  6  N - P
  7  R - S
  8  T - Z
  9  LIST ALL MERCHANTS
```

Fig. 7.5 *The menu that appears when you shop by merchant.*

Choose the appropriate letter range by typing the corresponding number. Choose option 5, for example, if you are looking for the MacWarehouse. To list all merchants, choose option 9.

Predictably, a list of all merchants is long; therefore, if you choose option 9, LIST ALL MERCHANTS, capture the list to disk or print it so that you can refer to it quickly to save time while logged on: remember, in CompuServe, time really *is* money.

After you choose the appropriate option, a listing of the merchants whose names begin with the specified letters appears (see fig. 7.6).

```
MALL (FREE)
  1 HOW TO USE THIS GUIDE
  2 JCPENNEY ONLINE CATALOG  [JCP]
     Apparel, electronics & merchandise
     VI/MC/AM/SC                        US
  3 LASER'S EDGE, THE  [LE]
     Laserdiscs and laser disc equipment
     VI/MC/DIS              US/CD/JP/OT
  4 LINCOLN/MERCURY SHOWROOM  [LM]
     Car information and dealer locator
     VI/MC                     US/CD
  5 MACUSER  [MC]
     Save 58% and Receive Free Gift
     VI/MC/DB                  US/CD
  6 MACWAREHOUSE  [MW]
     Macintosh hardware, software & access
     VI/MC/COD             US/CD/JP/OT
  7 MARYMAC INDUSTRIES  [MM]
     Official Radio Shack dealer
     VI/MC/AM/DIS/CSH          US/CD/JP
MORE !
```

Fig. 7.6 *A list of merchants beginning with the specified letters.*

The MORE ! prompt indicates that not all items on the list have been displayed. Press Enter to see additional merchants. When you find the merchant you want to visit, type the number of the merchant and press Enter. A greeting followed by the merchant's menu appears.

Shopping by Product

If you have a specific product or type of product in mind and want to locate one or more merchants that offer the product, use the product index. Choose option 3, Product Category Index, from the SHOP THE MALL menu. The Mall Product Index menu appears (see fig. 7.7). Access the index by choosing option 1, Index. The category list, shown in figure 7.8, appears.

```
Mall Product Index(FREE)    INX-1
MALL PRODUCT & INFORMATION INDEX
 1 Index
 2 How To Use the Index
 3 Suggestions On the Index
```

Fig. 7.7 The Mall Product Index menu.

```
Mall Product Index(FREE)    INX-5
PICK A CATEGORY
 1 Apparel/Accessories
 2 Audio Equipment
 3 Automotive
 4 Books
 5 Business Services
 6 Cameras/Optical Equipment
 7 Children's Clothes/Merchandise
 8 Collectibles
 9 Computer Hardware
10 Computer Peripherals/Accessories
MORE !
```

Fig. 7.8 The category list.

More categories exist (about 28 at present). You can see them by pressing Enter at the MORE ! prompt. When you find a category that interests you, enter the number of the category and press Enter to display a menu that breaks down the category further. For example, the menu shown in figure 7.9 appears when you choose option 21, Magazines/Periodicals/Catalogs.

```
Mall Product Index(FREE)   INX-34
MAGAZINES/PERIODICALS/
 CATALOGS
  1 Business
  2 Computer/Electronics
  3 General Interest
  4 Hobbies
  5 Kids
  6 News
```

Fig. 7.9 *The menu that appears when you choose option 21, Magazines/Periodicals/Catalogs.*

Type the number of the subcategory you need and press Enter. When you choose the subcategory (or the category itself when no subcategories are provided), a listing of merchants appears (see fig. 7.10).

```
Mall Product Index(FREE)
Category: Magazines/Periodicals/Catalogs
  1 Dow Jones & Co.           (DJ)
  2 Money's Financial Market  (MFM)
  3 PC Publications           (PCB)
  4 USA Today                 (UT)
```

Fig. 7.10 *A listing of merchants for the specified category.*

To the left of the merchant name is the menu option you choose to enter that merchant's store. To the right, in parentheses, is the GO code you can use at any ! prompt to enter a store. To reach PC Publications, for example, type **go pcb** at the ! prompt.

Understanding the Merchant Listing

The entry for each merchant—in the alphabetical listing (if you shop by merchant) or the department listing (if you shop by department)—uses codes with which you should be familiar. These codes are available any time you see the merchant entry. Consider, for example, the following entry for Barnes & Noble:

```
2 BARNES & NOBLE   [BN]
      America's Best Source for Books
      VI/MC/AM/DI/CSH          US/CD/JP/OT
```

The components of the Barnes & Noble entry are explained in the following:

- *[BN].* This item is the GO code. You can type **go bn** at any ! prompt to enter this merchant's store even if you're not in the Mall. Suppose, for example, that after reading messages in the Issues forum, you decide to look for and order a book mentioned on the message board. You can type **go bn** and press Enter to proceed directly to Barnes & Noble, bypassing the Mall menus.

- *VI/MC/AM/DI/CSH.* As you may assume, these codes indicate methods of payment accepted by the merchant. Table 7.1 describes the codes for payment methods that you can use in the Mall.

- *US/CD/JP/OT.* These codes indicate the countries to which the merchant is able to ship. The following list describes the codes that may appear:

Code	Country
US	United States
CD	Canada
JP	Japan
OT	Other (check with merchant for information)

Table 7.1 Payment Method Codes

Code	Payment Method
AM	American Express
COD	Cash on delivery
CSH	Cash, check, or money order (orders paid for in this way are processed by mail, not on-line)
DB	Direct bill
DI	Diners Club
DIS	Discover Card
MC	MasterCard
NA	Not applicable (a few merchants advertise in the Mall but do not allow you to make purchases)
SC	Store card (the merchant's credit card—the JC Penney card, for example)
VI	VISA

Ordering Products

When you enter a store, a greeting followed by the merchant's menu appears. Although these menus vary from merchant to merchant, the WaldenCOMPUTERBooks menu, shown in figure 7.11, is fairly typical.

```
WaldenCOMPUTERBooks(FREE)    WB-4
 1 Greetings
 2 ** THIS MONTH'S BEST SELLERS **
 3 ** HOT OFF THE PRESS **
 4 ** UPCOMING TITLES **
 5 ** SHOP IN OUR STORE **
   (Select from over 1000 titles)
 6 As Seen In CompuServe Magazine - December
 7 ** FOR ADVANCED USERS ONLY **
 8 Customer Service/Shipping Information
 9 Add Me to The Electronic Mailing List
10 *** AS SEEN IN GO MALL ***
```

Fig. 7.11 The WaldenCOMPUTERBooks menu.

All merchant menus provide an option that enables you to find out about the merchant's policies. In the WaldenCOMPUTERBooks menu, the option is number 8, Customer Service/Shipping Information. Within this option, many merchants also enable you to communicate on-line with them by typing and sending a message.

In addition, most merchants provide an option that enables you to subscribe to an electronic mailing list (option 9 in the WaldenCOMPUTERBooks menu). After you choose this option, CompuServe prompts you for your user ID number. Type your number and press Enter; the merchant's electronic mailings appear (see fig. 7.12).

```
WaldenCOMPUTERBooks(FREE)  WB-52
If you would like to be added to our
  Electronic Mailing list,
please enter your User I.D. here
User I.D.: 90611,555
Thank you!
% All responses correct (Y or N) ? y
```

Fig. 7.12 *The electronic mailing for the specified merchant.*

Special options are usually offered. In the Walden-COMPUTERBooks menu, for example, the special options are 2, 3, and 4. Option 2, This Month's Best Sellers, enables you to view a menu listing the best sellers according to Waldenbook's sales. You can order a book by typing the number to its left and pressing Enter.

Merchants also provide an option that enables you to shop in their store. In this case, the option is number 5, Shop in Our Store. Choosing this option normally produces a category list in the form of a menu, as shown in figure 7.13.

```
WaldenCOMPUTERBooks(FREE)   WB-12
  1 General Interest
  2 Hardware - Computer Specific
  3 Programming / Languages
  4 Operating Systems
  5 Spreadsheets
  6 Databases
  7 Integrated Software Packages
  8 Business Applications
  9 Word processing / Desktop Publishing
 10 Telecommunications
 11 Adv. Applications / Tech. Books
 12 Computer Accessories
```

Fig. 7.13 *A list of categories.*

Choose the appropriate category by typing the number and pressing Enter. A subcategory list or a listing of products appears (see fig. 7.14). From this list, you choose a category of products. To list *all* Macintosh related titles, for example, type **3**; information related to the specified category appears on-screen (see fig. 7.15).

```
WaldenCOMPUTERBooks(FREE)   WB-22
HARDWARE - COMPUTER SPECIFIC
  1 IBM
  2 Mainframes
  3 Macintosh
  4 Apple
  5 Amiga
  6 Printers
  7 Other Hardware
```

Fig. 7.14 *A product list.*

```
WaldenCOMPUTERBooks(FREE)       WB

 1 -- BACKLIST TITLES --
 2 10 Minute Guide to the Macintosh
 3 Apple Macintosh Book, 3rd Ed.
 4 Big Mac Book, 2/E
 5 Complete Book of HyperTalk 2
 6 Complete HyperCard 2.0 Handbook,
   3rd Edition
 7 Debugging Macintosh Software with
   MacsBug
 8 Designing and Writing Online
   Documentation
 9 HyperCard Script Language Guide
10 Inside Macintosh Communications Toolbox
11 Inside Macintosh Vol. I
12 Inside Macintosh Vol. II
13 Inside Macintosh Vol. III
14 Inside Macintosh Vol. IV
15 Inside Macintosh Vol. V
16 Inside Macintosh Vol. VI
17 Inside Macintosh X-Ref, Revised Edition
18 Inside the Macintosh
19 Little Mac Book, 2/E
20 Little QuicKeys Book
MORE !
```

Fig. 7.15 *Products relating to the specified category.*

After the list of products is displayed, you can choose a
product by typing its number. When you choose a product,
the product description appears (see fig. 7.16).

```
WaldenCOMPUTERBooks(FREE)

Que's Mac Classic Book

Author: Mark Bilbo

This book comprehensively introduces Apple's
newest and most popular Macintosh model. Step-
by-step instructions make sure users get up and
running with this low cost, easy-to-use machine.
The book offers lots of performance tips and
power-user techniques for business and home use.
Includes a complete command reference for vital
Mac Classic operations. Covers: setting up the
Macintosh; using the Desktop; managing files;
working with applications; integrating applica-
tions; and customizing the Mac.  500 pp.

Publisher: Que, 11/91 ISBN: 0880227702 Price:
$24.95

Last page. Enter "0" to order!
```

Fig. 7.16 A description of the selected product.

At the appropriate prompt, type **o** to order the product; type **r** if you do not want to order this item. If you type **o** and press Enter, you are prompted for the quantity of the item you want to order. Type the appropriate number and press Enter.

You do not have to enter your credit card number or complete the order at this point because shopping through CompuServe is similar to more traditional shopping; you can continue browsing, selecting additional items as desired, until you are ready to "check out."

After you select all items you plan to order, type **checkout** at the ! prompt. An order summary and prompt asking you to confirm your order appears (see fig. 7.17).

```
ORDER SUMMARY
You have ordered the following:
  1.  Que's Mac Classic Book
      (1)         24.95
TOTAL           24.95
NOTE: Total excludes tax and any
      other applicable charges.
Is this order correct? (Y/N) y
```

Fig. 7.17 The order summary and confirmation prompt.

Type **y** at the Is this order correct? prompt if the order is indeed what you want to purchase; however, if the order is incorrect or you want to change it, type **n** to display a menu that enables you to change your order. Keep in mind that you can type **exit** at any ! prompt to cancel your order.

When you check out, you are asked for your name, address, billing method (VISA, MasterCard, COD, and so forth), and other pertinent information. The information needed and the order in which it is requested depends on the merchant. At this point, however, you should have your credit card handy (unless the merchant does direct billing or COD).

Using Shopper's Advantage

Shopper's Advantage is an on-line equivalent of the discount house. You pay a membership to join, but after joining, you can order many brand name products at discount prices. (To join, you must use a major credit card.)

Accessing Shopper's Advantage

To access Shopper's Advantage, choose option 5 from the Mall's main menu or type **go sac** at any ! prompt. The SHOPPER'S ADVANTAGE menu appears (see fig. 7.18).

```
SHOPPERS ADVANTAGE
 (FREE CONNECT TIME)
 1 All About Us
 2 Shopping/Ordering for Members Only
 3 Browsing for Non-Members
 4 How To Join
 5 FREE Best Buys Catalog
   Shoppers Advantage HotLine
  (Customer Service/Help Desk)
       1-800-843-7777
```

Fig. 7.18 The SHOPPERS ADVANTAGE menu.

The SHOPPERS ADVANTAGE menu provides the following options:

■ *1 All About Us.* This option displays information about the Shopper's Advantage Club.

■ *2 Shopping/Ordering for Members Only.* This option enables members to shop and place orders.

■ *3 Browsing for Non-Members.* This option enables non-members to view products and prices but not place orders.

■ *4 How To Join.* This option explains club membership and enables you to join Shopper's Advantage. You must have your VISA or MasterCard handy to join.

■ *5 FREE Best Buys Catalog.* This option enables you to order the Best Buys Catalog.

Shopping with Shopper's Advantage

If you are a member, choose option 2, Shopping/Ordering for Members Only. You are prompted for your membership number. If you are not a member but want to view what the club has to offer, choose option 3, Browsing for Non-Members. The MAIN DIRECTORY menu appears (see fig. 7.19).

```
MAIN DIRECTORY              TOP
    1 All About Us
    2 What's New
    3 Best Buys
    4 Department Store
    5 Shop by Model #
    6 Shop by Product Category
    7 Shop by Product Code
    8 Info/Member Feedback
    9 Other Services
   10 Researching a Product
   11 Bridal Registry
   12 IdeaQuest Reward Program
   13 Holiday Return Policy
Enter choice :
```

Fig. 7.19 *The Shopper's Advantage MAIN DIRECTORY menu.*

The basic concepts of Shopper's Advantage are similar to those of the Electronic Mall except that you are dealing with only one merchant instead of many. Option 4, Department Store, presents merchandise in familiar, department store categories and is perhaps the easiest method to use. If you want the merchandise presented in general categories, choose option 6, Shop by Product Category. Alternatively, you may shop by model number (option 5) or product code (option 7).

Using Shopper's Advantage Commands

The membership kit you receive when you join the Shopper's Advantage Club explains the organization and how to use the club. Table 7.2 summarizes the commands that are available only in the Shopper's Advantage Club area.

Table 7.2 Shopper's Advantage Club Commands

Command (abbr)	Meaning
ADDRESS	Go to address change area
BACK (B)	Back up one screen or prompt
CANCEL	Cancel order placed in current session
CHANGE	Return to Department Store directory or change the product type selection
CHECKOUT	Complete order
COMPARE	Create a subset of selected products for review
DISPLAY	Display the current order
ENROLL	Go to the membership area to enroll
EXIT	Return to CompuServe
GO BEST	Enter "Best Buys" shopping
GO CODE	Shop by product code
GO DEPT	Go to the department store
GO HOME	Go to home furnishings ordering information
GO INFO	Go to Info/Member feedback area
GO MAIN	Go to the main directory
GO MEMBER	Go to the address change area
GO NEW	Go to the What's New area
GO OTHER	Move to Other Services directory
HELP (H)	Display all commands
LIST	Display product and brand name choices
MENU (M)	Move to preceding menu or directory
NP	Narrow product selection by responding to descriptive questions
OFF, BYE	Exit Shopper's Advantage and CompuServe (log off)
P#	Enter additional page selections for viewing products
REDISPLAY (R)	Redisplay current directory or prompt
SCROLL (S)	Change screen display to scroll text

Command (abbr)	Meaning
SCROLL OFF	Change the screen display to page mode
SHIP	Change the ship-to address for an order
TOP (T)	Go to the main directory

Using Softex

Softex is CompuServe's on-line software catalog and ordering system. Softex enables you to order software and download it directly to your computer.

Accessing and Shopping on Softex

To access Softex, type **go softex** at any ! prompt. When you enter Softex, the SOFTEX menu appears (see fig. 7.20).

```
CompuServe                    SOFTEX
Welcome to SOFTEX, CompuServe's
 Online Software Catalog.
 1 Introduction to SOFTEX(sm)
 2 Instructions for Searching
 3 Search SOFTEX Catalog (W)
 4 Featured Selections (W)
 5 Talk to the SOFTEX Manager
 6 What's New in SOFTEX
```

Fig. 7.20 *The SOFTEX menu.*

The SOFTEX menu offers the following options:

- *1 Introduction to SOFTEX.* This option explains Softex and the basics of using Softex.

- *2 Instructions for Searching.* This option describes how you can search for software in Softex.

■ *3 Search SOFTEX Catalog (W).* This option enables you to begin a search of the Softex catalog.

■ *4 Featured Selections (W).* This option displays a menu of the featured products.

■ *5 Talk to the SOFTEX Manager.* This option enables you to leave a mail message for the manager.

■ *6 What's New in SOFTEX.* This option produces a menu of new products.

If you choose option 3, Search *SOFTEX* Catalog, the Search menu appears (see fig. 7.21).

```
CompuServe
Search by:
 1 Computer Model
 2 Software Category
 3 Publisher
 4 Software Title
 5 SOFTEX Catalog Number
 6 New/Updated Selections
```

Fig. 7.21 *The Softex Search menu.*

The following options are available on the Search menu:

■ *1 Computer Model.* This option presents a list of computers from which you can choose.

■ *2 Software Category.* This option displays software categories from which you can choose.

■ *3 Publisher.* This option presents a list of software publishers from which you can choose.

■ *4 Software Title.* This option prompts you for a program name to search for.

■ *5 SOFTEX Catalog Number.* This option prompts you for a catalog number to search for.

■ *6 New/Updated Selections.* This option lists new products and updates.

Downloading from Softex

After you choose a software title to purchase, a prompt appears, asking you for the transfer protocol your communications package can handle (you can find this information in your manual). Choose the protocol and issue the command that enables your communications package to receive downloads.

CompuServe indicates how long downloading the program will take, and the software company usually mails the software manuals to you. The charge for the software appears on your CompuServe bill. *Note:* Connect time is not waived in Softex. In a way, it is the "shipping charge" for the program.

Using Travel Services

CompuServe offers several travel-related services that can help you plan a trip. The services include EAASY SABRE, OAG EE (the Official Airlines Guide Electronic Edition), and ABC (ABC Worldwide Hotel Guide). Through these services, you can check airline schedules, reserve seats, book hotel rooms, rent cars, and perform other useful travel-related functions.

Using EAASY SABRE

EAASY SABRE is offered by American Airlines and is not actually a part of the CompuServe Information System. Consequently, the normal CompuServe commands with which you are familiar do not function. This section serves as a guide to using the commands specific to EAASY SABRE.

Accessing EAASY SABRE

You access EAASY SABRE by typing **go eaasy** at any exclamation mark (!) prompt. You also can choose option 5, Travel, from the TOP menu. Then choose option 1, Air Information/Reservations, from the Travel menu. When the Travel

Services Flights menu appears, choose option 1, EAASY
SABRE. The EAASY SABRE menu, shown in figure 8.1,
appears.

```
EAASY SABRE
 1 Introduction
 2 How to Use
 3 What is EAASY SABRE (CIM)
 4 Bargain Finder
 5 Talk to EAASY SABRE
 6 Talk to Travelers Access
 7 Access EAASY SABRE
 8 Access EAASY SABRE (CIM)
** HELP DESK 800-331-2690 **
```

Fig. 8.1 *The EAASY SABRE menu.*

The EAASY SABRE menu provides the following options:

- *1 Introduction.* This option displays an introduction
  to EAASY SABRE.

- *2 How to Use.* This option explains how to use EAASY
  SABRE.

- *3 What is EAASY SABRE (CIM).* This option explains
  EAASY SABRE CIM, the new interface for EAASY SA-
  BRE (see Chapter 11, "Using the CompuServe Infor-
  mation Manager," for more information about CIM).

- *4 Bargain Finder.* This option explains the use of the
  Bargain Finder feature of EAASY SABRE.

- *5 Talk to EAASY SABRE.* This option enables you to
  leave a message for EAASY SABRE operators.

- *6 Talk to Travelers Access.* This option enables you
  to leave a message for Travelers Access.

- *7 Access EAASY SABRE.* This option enables you to
  access EAASY SABRE if you are not using CIM.

- *8 Access EAASY SABRE (CIM).* This option enables you
  to access EAASY SABRE if you are using CIM.

Applying to EAASY SABRE

Applying to use EAASY SABRE is free and gives you a unique AAdvantage number, an EAASY SABRE user guide, an on-line profile specifying your personal travel preferences, the capability to use EAASY SABRE for itinerary planning, and other options.

To apply to EAASY SABRE, do the following:

1. Choose option 7, Access EAASY SABRE, from the EAASY SABRE menu. An introductory message appears asking you to enter your AAdvantage number.

2. Because you do not have an AAdvantage number at this point, press Enter. The EAASY SABRE MAIN MENU appears.

3. Choose option 5, Application to use EAASY SABRE.

4. Type your name, address, telephone number, and other information at the appropriate prompts to complete the application.

You are issued an AAdvantage number; then you can assign a password of your choice.

You can press Enter instead of performing steps 3 and 4 if you do not want to apply for an AAdvantage number. Without an AAdvantage number, however, not all EAASY SABRE functions are available to you, although you still can browse flight information.

Signing On to EAASY SABRE

After you have your AAdvantage number and password, use the following process to sign on to EAASY SABRE:

1. Choose option 7, Access EAASY SABRE, from the EAASY SABRE menu.

2. Type /**signon**, *aadvantage number, password*. (Insert your AAdvantage number and password.) The EAASY SABRE MAIN MENU appears.

Checking Flight Information

To check flight information and make reservations, sign on
to EAASY SABRE as described in the preceding section. The
EAASY SABRE MAIN MENU, shown in figure 8.2, appears.

```
EAASY SABRE MAIN MENU

                     AAdvantage Number: ABC1234

 1  System Quick Tips                  6  Profile Review and Change

 2  Travel Reservations and Information  7  Travelers Access

 3  Weather Information                8  Official Recreation Guide

 4  AAdvantage                        9  Sign Off

 5  Application to use EAASY SABRE

To select one of the options above, enter the number:

** Quick Tip:  These system navigation commands are always available:

    Help or  ? for assistance

    Res  or /R to go to the Reservations Menu

    Top  or /T to return to the Main Menu

    Exit or /E to return to your System Operator
```

Fig. 8.2 *The EAASY SABRE MAIN MENU.*

Choose option 2, Travel Reservations and Information,
to check flight information. The RESERVATIONS MENU
appears (see fig. 8.3).

To check on flights and make reservations, follow these
steps:

1. Choose option 1, Flight Reservations and Availability,
    from the RESERVATIONS MENU.

    A prompt appears, asking you for the city of
    departure.

2. Type the name of the city and press Enter. Alterna-
    tively, you can enter the airport's three letter code
    (you may have seen these codes used on airline
    tickets and baggage tags—LAX for Los Angeles, IAH
    for Houston Intercontinental, and so forth).

```
RESERVATIONS MENU
1  Flight Reservations and Availability    5  Airline Fares
2  Flight Arrival/Departure Information     6  Itinerary Review and
                                               Change
3  Hotels                                   7  Sign On another User
4  Rental Cars                              8  Flight Schedules
                                            9  Specific Flight Details
To select one of the options above, enter the number:
Quick Tip: The following system navigation commands are always
available:
Help or ? for assistance, or
Res or /R to return to this menu or
Top or /T to return to the MAIN MENU or
Exit or /E to return to the System Operator
```

Fig. 8.3 *The RESERVATIONS MENU.*

If a city has more than one airport, a menu of airports appears. Choose the airport you plan to use. A prompt appears, asking you for the city (or airport code) of your destination.

3. Enter the city you plan to travel to (or the airport code) and press Enter.

   If the city you plan to travel to has more than one airport, you are asked to indicate which airport you want to use (unless you used the airport code). To specify the appropriate airport, choose the airport from the menu.

4. Enter the date you plan to travel and press Enter. Use three letters for the month and two numbers for the date—for example, *Jan 01*, *Feb 19*, *Oct 02*.

   The menu shown in figure 8.4 appears.

```
You may customize the display of available
flights by selecting one or more
options:
  1  Show only flights with a specific class
     of service available
  2  Show only flights for a specific airline
  3  Show availability for a specific airline
     and flight number
  4  Show only flights connecting via a
     specific city
  5  Schedules displayed based on arrival
     time
Example:  2  or  1,3
Or press <ENTER> to view all available
flights.
```

Fig. 8.4 *The menu that appears after you enter destination and date information.*

5. To view all available flights, press Enter; otherwise, choose the desired option and press Enter.

   If you choose one of these options, you are asked to specify your selection. If this is too confusing, simply press Enter to show all available flights.

6. Enter the departure time and press Enter. Use no colons and only *A* and *P* to indicate A.M. and P.M., respectively. For example, you enter 8:00 A.M. as *800A* and 6:30 P.M. as *630P*.

   The FLIGHT AVAILABILITY menu, which is explained in the section "Using the FLIGHT AVAILABILITY Menu," appears.

Using Quickpath Options

Rather than using all the steps listed in the preceding section to specify your departure and destination information, you can use *Quickpath* options, which enable you to enter this information on one line. When you are prompted for your city of departure after choosing option 1, Flight

Reservations and Availability, you can enter the information in the following format:

departure city,destination city,travel date,departure time

To use Quickpath to request information for flights between Houston Intercontinental and Long Beach on February 1st, departing on or about 8 A.M., for example, you enter the following (be sure to separate each item with commas):

    IAH,LGB,Feb01,800A

After you enter this information, the FLIGHT AVAILABILITY menu, explained in the next section, appears.

8

Using the FLIGHT AVAILABILITY Menu

After you enter the travel information at the appropriate prompts or the one line Quickpath information, the FLIGHT AVAILABILITY menu appears (see fig. 8.5).

```
FLIGHT AVAILABILITY
From:  (IAH) INTERCONTINENTAL-HOU
  To:  (LGB) LONG BEACH, CA                    SATURDAY  FEB-01-92
.............................................
  Flight   Leave      Arrive   Meal Stop Aircraft OnTime  Classes of Service**
1 AA   5  IAH  725A  DFW  832A       0    S80      8      F  Y  B  M  Q  H  V  K
  AA 461        922A  LGB 1045A  R    0    S80      6      F  Y  B  M  H  Q  V  K
2 AA 395  IAH  900A  DFW 1008A       0    72S      8      F  Y  B  M  Q  H  V  K
  AA1439       1107A  LGB 1232P  L    0    S80      8      F  Y  B  M  H  Q  V  K
3 HP 484  IAH  640A  PHX  834A  S    0    733      9      F  Y  B  H  K  Q  V  M
  HP 830        929A  LGB  950A       0    733      8      Y  B  H  K  Q  V  M
.............................................
To SELECT a flight, enter the line number, or
  8  View MORE flights              11  View all FARES
  9  CHANGE flight request          12  Translate CODES
 10  View FIRST flight display      13  View LOWest one-way fares
** Quick Tip:  Select your flight, then choose Bargain Finder when
prompted and EAASY SABRE will select the class of service for the
lowest available fare.
```

Fig. 8.5 *The FLIGHT AVAILABILITY menu.*

The menu shown in figure 8.5 lists February 1st flights that depart on or about 8 A.M. from Houston, Texas, and arrive in Long Beach, California. The items in this list are explained in the following:

- *Flight.* The airline and flight number. AA 5 is American Airlines flight 5.

- *Leave.* Departure airport and time. IAH 725A indicates Houston Intercontinental airport, and 7:25 A.M. is the departure time, for example.

- *Arrive.* Arrival airport and time. DFW 832A indicates that the flight arrives in Dallas-Ft. Worth at 8:32 A.M., for example.

- *Meal.* Meal type. This item is blank if no meal is provided.

- *Stop.* Number of stops made by this flight.

- *Aircraft.* Aircraft type.

- *On Time.* On-time rating, which indicates how often the flight is on time. For example, 8 represents an 80 to 89 percent on-time rating.

- *Classes of Service.* The classes of service offered on this flight.

To reserve the flight, you enter the number to the left of a flight (enter **1** to reserve flight AA 5, for example). You also can use the menu options, explained below, to obtain additional information:

- *8 View MORE flights.* This option lists additional flights that match the specified arrival and departure information.

- *9 CHANGE flight request.* This option enables you to enter another travel request.

- *10 View FIRST flight display.* This option displays the first flight display you viewed.

- *11 View all FARES.* This option enables you to view fare information for the flights.

■ *12 Translate CODES.* This option enables you to find the meaning of an airport code, airline code, aircraft code, and so forth. You also may do the reverse—that is, enter a city and obtain its airport codes, for example.

■ *13 View LOWest one-way fares.* This option displays the lowest one-way fares.

Reserving a Flight

To make reservations, you must sign on with your AAdvantage number. When you see the flight that you want to reserve in the FLIGHT AVAILABILITY menu, you choose the number to the left of the flight information line. Information about the flight appears, and you are offered the option to use the Bargain Finder feature to locate the lowest fare.

At this point, you can make other air travel reservations or reservations for hotel rooms and rental cars. You also are asked whether you want to make a return reservation.

Changing a Reservation

You can change or cancel reservations by choosing option 6, Itinerary Review and Change, from the RESERVATIONS MENU (refer to fig. 8.3). A listing of your itinerary appears. Choose the item you want to change or cancel; then you are prompted to verify any changes.

Using OAG EE

The Official Airlines Guide Electronic Edition (OAG EE) is an independent information and reservation system that is not affiliated with any airline. When you use this system, you incur a surcharge in addition to the usual network and connection fees you pay to use CompuServe. Using the OAG, you can view flight information, book flights, and arrange for ticketing, as well as access various travel information systems. Presently, the OAG database is updated and used by 413 airlines for scheduling information.

Accessing OAG EE

To access OAG EE, type **go oag** at any ! prompt. The OAG
ELECTRONIC EDITION TRAVEL SERVICE menu—OAG
menu, for short—appears (see fig. 8.6).

```
CompuServe                      OAG-1
OAG ELECTRONIC EDITION TRAVEL SERVICE
 1 Description
 2 Command summary
 3 Feedback
 4 New Travel Agency Ticketing Outlets
 5 Access ($)
OAG Help Desk:
     U.S.A.   800/323-4000
     Outside U.S.A  708/574-6414
```

Fig. 8.6 The OAG menu.

The options available on the OAG menu are explained in
the following:

■ *1 Description.* This option describes the OAG EE
service.

■ *2 Command summary.* This option lists the available
OAG EE commands.

■ *3 Feedback.* This option enables you to comment on
OAG EE.

■ *4 New Travel Agency Ticketing Outlets.* This option
lists new travel agencies from which you can purchase
tickets.

■ *5 Access ($).* This option enables you to access
OAG EE.

Enter the OAG EE service by choosing option 5, Access.

Using OAG EE Commands

Table 8.1 lists the commands you can use from any OAG EE prompt. When you use these commands, substitute the line number of the flight or fare for the pound symbol [#].

Table 8.1 OAG EE Commands

Command	Use To
Single line requests (examples follow the table):	
/C	Cancel or review bookings
/E	Turn expert mode on or off
/F	Initiate a fare request
/H	Initiate a hotel request
/I	Request information
/M	Display the command menu
/Q	Exit OAG EE
/S	Initiate a schedule request
/U	Send a message to OAG EE
Navigational commands used in searches:	
+	Move to the next screen
–	Move to the preceding screen
CX	Display flight connections
DF	Display direct flights
M	Go to fares or hotel menus
O	Display the original screen
RF	Display return fares
RS	Display return flights
Flight and fare information commands:	
A#	Display fares and seats available
B#	Book flight or connection
F#	Display fares offered on a specified flight
L#	Display fare restrictions

continues

Table 8.1 Continued

Command	Use To
S#	Display flights for your fare choice
X#	Display expanded information
Help command:	
?	Translate city codes or other codes (for example, typing *?IAH* displays IAH=Houston, TX, USA)
Other commands:	
MM	Return to the Main Menu
OFF	Exit OAG EE and return to CompuServe

To display the schedule of flights for Houston to Long Beach Jun 15 at 1 P.M., type the following (you can use city codes instead of city names):

    /S IAH;LGB;15JUN 1P

To display fares for flights between Houston and Long Beach on Jun 15, type this command:

    /F Houston;Long Beach 15JUN

Using the ABC Worldwide Hotel Guide

The ABC Worldwide Hotel Guide provides information about hotels throughout the world. You can find the location, rates, and facilities of literally tens of thousands of hotels by using this guide. To access the hotel guide, type **go abc** at any ! prompt. The ABC WORLDWIDE HOTEL GUIDE menu, shown in figure 8.7, appears.

```
CompuServe                ABC-1
ABC WORLDWIDE HOTEL GUIDE
 1 What is ABC Worldwide Hotel
    Guide?
 2 Worldwide Hotel Listings
 3 How to Use ABC Worldwide
    Hotel Guide
 4 List of Countries
 5 Feedback/Comments
```

Fig. 8.7 *The ABC WORLDWIDE HOTEL GUIDE menu.*

This menu provides the following options:

- *1 What is ABC Worldwide Hotel Guide?* This option explains the hotel guide.

- *2 Worldwide Hotel Listings.* This option enables you to access the hotel listings.

- *3 How to Use ABC Worldwide Hotel Guide.* This option explains how to use the guide.

- *4 List of Countries.* This option lists the countries for which hotel information is provided.

- *5 Feedback/Comments.* This option enables you to comment on the service.

To begin a hotel search, choose option 2, Worldwide Hotel Listings, from the ABC WORLDWIDE HOTEL GUIDE menu. A menu from which you choose the country or island containing hotel information you want to view appears.

Enter the number of the country and press Enter. You may then be asked to narrow your search. If you choose option 1, United States, for example, you are asked to type the name of the state to be searched. Enter as many letters as you need to specify a state. You can enter **okl** for Oklahoma, for instance. You usually must enter at least three letters so that the system can determine the appropriate state or province. Entering only **M** for a state in the U.S., for example, accesses information about Maine, Mississippi, Missouri, and so on.

If the list of hotels for the specified area is long, you can narrow the search by entering a city name at the appropriate prompt. Type at least the first three or four letters of the city's name and press Enter. Although you can press Enter to list all located hotels, this can result in a very long listing. If the list is still long, a menu such as the one shown in figure 8.8 appears.

```
CompuServe                    QKO-100
  1 Display Hotels List
  2 Narrow by Price Range
  3 Narrow by Exact Hotel Name
  4 Narrow by Hotel Chain
  5 Narrow by Location/Amenities
  6 Restore Previous Selection Set
  7 Begin a New Search
  8 Exit Search
```

Fig. 8.8 *Narrowing the search for hotels.*

This menu enables you to narrow your search by setting various conditions, explained in the following:

- *1 Display Hotels List.* This option displays all hotels found; it does not narrow the search.

- *2 Narrow by Price Range.* This option enables you to narrow the search so that only hotels in a certain price range are included.

- *3 Narrow by Exact Hotel Name.* This option enables you to eliminate all hotels except those matching a specified name.

■ *4 Narrow by Hotel Chain.* This option enables you to reduce the list to hotels of a specific chain.

■ *5 Narrow by Location/Amenities.* This option enables you to narrow the search, based on proximity to airports or other desired locales or amenities, such as Fax machines.

■ *6 Restore Previous Selection Set.* This option enables you to restore the last set of hotels. If you narrowed a search and find that it reduces the list too much, for example, choose this option to restore the preceding list.

■ *7 Begin a New Search.* This option displays the first hotel search menu so that you can begin an entirely new search.

■ *8 Exit Search.* This option enables you to leave the search and return to the Main Menu.

8

Using Financial Services

CompuServe offers a variety of services intended for people who need up-to-date information about the financial markets. Through CompuServe's financial services, you can access stock quotes, bond prices, SEC filings, annual reports, and many other kinds of information.

The most cost-efficient way to use CIS financial services is to first request the Executive Option for billing purposes. The Executive Option reduces the costs of accessing many financial services in exchange for a slightly higher monthly fee. Using the Executive Option is not mandatory; consider this option only if you frequently access financial services.

To add the Executive Option, type **go executive** at any command prompt. CompuServe presents a menu from which you can access information and instructions for adding the Executive Option to your account.

Finding Securities Symbols

To locate an issues ticker symbol or CUSIP number, type
go cusip at any ! prompt. The menu shown in figure 9.1
appears.

```
Search by:
 1 Name
 2 Ticker Symbol
 3 CUSIP Number
 4 CNUM
 5 Primary SIC Code
```

Fig. 9.1 *The menu you use to locate ticker symbols.*

When you type the number of the appropriate search option, CompuServe prompts you for the *search string* (letters or numbers you are searching for). If you are looking
for a particular company, for example, you would enter
the company name or its ticker symbol.

If you search by name and have trouble finding the issues
of a particular company, type **/help abbreviations** for an
explanation of common abbreviations used.

Finding Bonds

To locate issue identifiers for bonds, type **go bonds** at any
! prompt. CompuServe prompts you to enter the issuer's
ticker symbol or company name. Enter the ticker symbol
and press Enter or type an asterisk (*) followed by all or
part of the company name.

If you enter only part of a company name, a menu listing
all companies that match your entry appears. You choose
a company from this menu, which is similar to the menu
shown in figure 9.2.

```
Bonds Listing BONDS
Enter ticker symbols (i.e. DEC,IBM), an
asterisk followed by beginning of a company
name (i.e. *DIGITAL), /H for HELP or /EXIT.
Issuer: *Apple
Bonds Listing
    Ticker Company Name                   Issue
    ------ ------- ----                   -----
  1 APK    APPLE BANCORP INC              COM
  2 AAPL   APPLE COMPUTER INC             COM
  3 APSO   APPLE SOUTH INC                COM
  4 APPW   APPLE WEAR CO
  5 APPB   APPLEBEES INTL INC             COM
  6 APWD   APPLEWOODS RESTAURANTS INC     COM
```

Fig. 9.2 *Finding issues identifiers for bonds by choosing a company.*

Finding Market Indicators

You can locate interest rates, exchange rates, and market indicators through CompuServe's Market Indicator Review service. To access this service, type **go indicators** at any ! prompt; the COMMODITIES LIST menu, shown in figure 9.3, appears.

```
COMMODITIES LIST CSYMBOL
 1 List by Group
 2 List by Exchange
Enter Choice !
```

Fig. 9.3 *The COMMODITIES LIST menu.*

You can list commodities by group (type of commodity) or by the exchange on which the commodities are traded. If you choose option 1, List by Group, the Commodity Listing by Group menu appears (see fig. 9.4).

```
Commodity Listing by Group
 1 Currencies
 2 Fats/Oils
 3 Fiber
 4 Financial
 5 Foods
 6 Grains/Feeds
 7 Index
 8 Metals
 9 Petroleum
10 Woods
11 Fertilizers
Enter Choice !
```

Fig. 9.4 *The Commodity Listing by Group menu.*

Enter the number of the commodity you want to list and press Enter. A menu that further subdivides the commodity group appears; choose the appropriate commodity. After you choose a commodity, CompuServe prompts you for the settlement date, as shown in figure 9.5.

```
Settlement date (in form MMYY, e.g., 192):1091
COMMODITIES LIST
Long Symbol: NYNG        Short Symbol: NYNG
Description: Natural Gas
Delivered on: Oct  91
Exchange: NYME
First Pricing Date: 12/31/90
Last Pricing Date: 09/23/91
```

Fig. 9.5 *Entering the settlement date.*

Enter the settlement date in MMYY form (October 1991 is *1091*, for example) and press Enter.

Choose option 2, List by Exchange, from the COMMODI-TIES LIST menu to list commodity information by the exchange on which the commodity is traded. When you choose option 2, the Commodity Listing by Exchange menu appears (see fig. 9.6).

```
Commodity Listing by Exchange
 1 CASH    Cash Prices
 2 CBT     Chicago Board of Trade
 3 CEI     Commodity Exchange, New York
 4 CME     Chicago Mercantile Exchange
 5 CNS     Commodity News Service
 6 CRCE    Chicago Rice & Cotton Exchange
 7 CSCE    Coffee, Sugar & Cocoa Exchange
 8 CTN     New York Cotton Exchange
 9 IMM     International Monetary Market
10 IPE     International Petroleum Exchange
11 KCBT    Kansas City Board of Trade
12 LIFFE   London Intl Financial Futures
13 MCE     MidAmerica Commodity Exchange
14 MGE     Minneapolis Grain Exchange
15 NYFE    New York Futures Exchange
16 NYME    New York Mercantile Exchange
17 SFE     Sydney Futures Exchange
18 SIMEX   Singapore Futures Exchange
19 WPG     Winnipeg Commodity Exchange
Enter Choice !
```

Fig. 9.6 *The Commodity Listing by Exchange menu.*

Choose the exchange whose commodities you want to list. A menu appears, asking you to narrow your choice further. CompuServe then asks you to provide the settlement date.

Using Stock Market Services

CompuServe offers several services for users who deal with the stock market. You can obtain current quotes on stocks, options, market indicators, and so forth.

Getting Current Quotes

You can obtain quotes on stocks from CompuServe. These quotes are delayed a minimum of 15 minutes. To obtain a quote, type **go qquote** at any ! prompt.

A prompt appears, asking you for the ticker symbol. Enter the ticker symbol and press Enter. If you don't know the ticker symbol, you can enter a company name preceded by an asterisk (*). Figure 9.7 illustrates how you can obtain a quote for H&R Block.

```
Quick Quote QQUOTE

Quotes are delayed over 15 minutes.  CompuServe does not edit this
data and is not responsible or liable for its content, completeness,
or timeliness.

DOW 30 was down 21.47 on 1/31
Quotes are surcharged 1.5 cents each.
Enter ticker symbols (i.e. HRB,SP 500), an asterisk followed by
beginning of a company name (i.e. *BLOCK), /H for HELP or /EXIT.

Issue: HRB

Name              Volume   Hi/Ask   Low/Bid  Last    Change  Update
---------------- -------- ------- -------- ------- -------- ------
BLOCK H & R INC COM 3392  37.000   35.125   36.000  -0.625  1/31

Issue: /exit
```

Fig. 9.7 Getting a quick quote from H&R Block.

Type /**exit** to quit Qquote or /**help** (/**h**) to get help.

Getting Market Highlights

You can obtain reports of market highlights by typing **go market** at any ! prompt; the EXCHANGE menu appears (see fig. 9.8).

```
EXCHANGE
1 (N) New York Stock Exchange
2 (A) American Exchange
3 (O) Over the Counter
Enter choice!
```

Fig. 9.8 The EXCHANGE menu.

Choose the exchange for which you want to review highlights by typing the number and pressing Enter. A menu
listing the highlights of the preceding day appears (see
fig. 9.9).

```
Market Highlights
                        MOST ACTIVE STOCKS

           GAINS                              LOSSES

Updated  1/31          # of Cos    Updated  1/31          # of Cos

 1 20 Most Active Stocks    20     11 20 Largest Losses        20
 2 20 Largest Gains         20     12 20 Largest % Losses      20
 3 20 Largest % Gains       20     13 Price Down Past 3 Days  144
 4 Price Up Past 3 Days     76     14 Price Down Past 4 Days   63
 5 Price Up Past 4 Days     42     15 Price Down Past 5 Days   27
 6 Price Up Past 5 Days     19     16 New 6-Month Low           2
 7 New 6-Month High          4     17 High Below Yesterday     42
 8 Low Above Yesterday's Hi 86     18 Volume 2X Average & Down 77
 9 Volume 2X Average & Up   98     19 20 Largest $ Vol Losses  20
10 20 Largest $ Vol Gains   20
      Enter choices or ALL!
```

Fig. 9.9 Market highlights.

Enter the number of the item you want to display. To see
more than one item, enter the appropriate numbers separated by commas. Type **all** and press Enter to display all
options.

Getting General Company Information

Several services are combined in the Company Analyzer
service offered by CompuServe. You can access company
information, price histories, bond issues, and more. To access the service, type **go analyzer** at any ! prompt; the
ANALYZER menu, shown in figure 9.10, appears.

```
CompuServe                    ANALYZER
One moment please...
Company Analyzer ANALYZER
Data except for H&R Block (symbol HRB) is
surcharged.
Enter a ticker symbol (i.e. HRB), a company
name search (asterisk followed by beginning
of name, i.e. *BLOCK), /H for HELP or /EXIT.
Company:
```

Fig. 9.10 The ANALYZER menu.

Enter the ticker symbol for the company; if you don't know
the ticker symbol, enter the company name preceded by an
asterisk (*). Figure 9.11 shows an example of the analysis
options offered for H&R Block (H&R Block's ticker symbol
is HRB).

The menu options vary from company to company, depending on the available information. Choose the option
you want to view by entering the number displayed to the
left of the option and pressing Enter.

```
Company Analyzer

BLOCK H & R INC                 (HRB)          CUSIP number: 09367110

COM                                            Exchange: N

   Date     Time    Volume    High    Low     Last    Change

  .......   ....   ........   .....   ......  ......   ......

  1/31/92   0:01   339,200    37      35 1/8  36        -0 5/8

  1 Descriptive Company Profile   10 Management Discussion

  2 Price History from 6/25/79    11 Earnings/Growth Forecasts

  3 Dividends from 11/03/69       12 Officers, Directors, Salaries

  4 Price Stats, Last 52 Weeks    13 All Above Disclosure Reports

  5 Detailed Issue Description    14 Ownership

                                  15 Price Volume Graph

  7 Options Issued, Appx 36

  8 Return on $1000 Invested          No News Today for HRB

  9 Financial Statements

  !
```

Fig. 9.11 H&R Block analysis options.

Using Other Services

This section covers three services of CompuServe that do not fall into any other category: the games, the weather service, and the nationwide classified ads service.

Using Games

CompuServe offers numerous games, from standard board games to interactive game show-type games that you can play with many other users. Of course, covering all these games in this book is impossible; instead, this section is a guide to help you explore the games section.

Accessing Games

To move to the Entertainment/Games menu, shown in figure 10.1, type **go games** at any exclamation mark (!) prompt.

This menu offers the following options:

■ *1 Intro to Games.* This option displays a menu that enables you to obtain general information about games.

■ *2 Fantasy/Role Playing/Adventures.* This option enables you to choose a role-playing game from a menu.

■ *3 War/Simulation Games.* This option displays the menu of war and other simulation games.

■ *4 Parlor/Trivia Games.* This option enables you to access the menu of board and trivia games.

■ *5 Modem Games and Challenge Board.* This option enables you to choose one of the interactive games from a menu and to access the challenge board where members can post challenges.

■ *6 Game Forums/News.* This option displays a menu from which you can access one of the gaming forums or obtain gaming news (such as announcements of the times for on-line interactive games).

■ *7 Entertainment Forums.* This option displays a menu of the entertainment forums that are not dedicated entirely to gaming but contain a section or library related to games.

■ *8 Entertainment News.* This option enables you to access entertainment news items.

■ *9 Order Merchandise/Guides.* This option enables you to order game-related merchandise and printed guides.

```
Entertainment/Games          GAMES
  1 Intro to Games
  2 Fantasy/Role Playing/Adventures
  3 War/Simulation Games
  4 Parlor/Trivia Games
  5 Modem Games and Challenge Board
  6 Game Forums/News
  7 Entertainment Forums
  8 Entertainment News
  9 Order Merchandise/Guides
```

Fig. 10.1 The Entertainment/Games menu.

Using Quick Reference Words

You can access games, game forums, or game news by typing **go** followed by one of the quick reference words at any ! prompt. Tables 10.1 and 10.2 list the quick reference words.

Table 10.1 Quick Reference Words for Games

Quick Ref. Word	Game
ADVENT	Fantasy/Role-playing/Adventure
ASTROLOGY	Astrological Charting
ATCONTROL	Air Traffic Controller
BIORHYTHMS	Biorhythm Charting
BLACKDRAGON	BlackDragon
CLADVENT	Classic Adventure
CQUEST	CastleQuest
EGAMER	The Electronic Gamer
ENADVENT	Enhanced Adventure
HANGMAN	Hangman
ISLAND	Island of Kesmai
LEGENDS	British Legends
MEGA1	MegaWars I
MEGA3	MegaWars III
MTMLOBBY	Modem to Modem Game Lobby
MULTIPLECHOICE	The Multiple Choice
SEAWAR	SeaWAR
SGAMES	Space Games
SHOWBIZ	SHOWBIZQUIZ
SNIPER	SNIPER
TTGAMES	Parlor/Trivia Games
WARGAMES	War Games
WHIZ	The Whiz Quiz
YGI	You Guessed It!

Table 10.2 Quick Reference Words for News

Quick Ref. Word	Forum/News
CHALLENGE	Modem Players Challenge Board
GAMECON	Game Forums/News
GAMERS	The Gamers Forum
MPGAMES	The Multi-Player Games Forum
MTMFORUM	Modem Games Forum
MTMGAMES	Modem to Modem Game Support
PBMGAMES	Play-By-Mail Forum
RPGAMES	Role-Playing Games Forum

Obtaining Weather Reports

Through CompuServe, you can obtain weather reports that are updated by the FAA and the National Weather Service. Local forecasts, aviation weather reports, and weather maps are available. Global weather reports are soon to be added.

Accessing Weather Reports

To access the weather report options, type **go weather** at any ! prompt. The WEATHER menu, shown in figure 10.2, appears.

```
News/Weather/Sports        WEATHER
WEATHER
  1 Weather Reports
  2 Weather Maps
  3 NWS Aviation Weather
  4 Associated Press Online
  5 UK Weather
  6 Global Weather Coming Soon
```

Fig. 10.2 *The WEATHER menu.*

This menu offers the following options:

■ *1 Weather Reports.* This option enables you to access the local and state weather forecasts.

■ *2 Weather Maps.* This option enables you to request weather maps, including satellite maps; however, you must have a communications package such as Navigator or a graphics package that can handle RLE graphics.

■ *3 NWS Aviation Weather.* This option enables you to obtain aviation weather forecasts.

■ *4 Associated Press Online.* This option enables you to obtain Associated Press weather news.

■ *5 UK Weather.* This option enables you to obtain United Kingdom weather reports.

■ *6 Global Weather Coming Soon.* This option explains the coming global weather information services.

Obtaining a Local Forecast

Choose option 1, Weather Reports, from the WEATHER menu to display the WEATHER REPORTS menu that enables you to access local forecasts (see fig. 10.3).

```
WEATHER REPORTS
 1 (SF) Short Term Forecasts
 2 (EF) Extended Forecasts
 3 (SW) Severe Weather Alerts
 4 (PP) Precipitation Probability
 5 (SS) State Summaries
 6 (CL) Daily Climatological Reports
 7 (SP) Sports and Recreation
 8 (MF) Marine Forecasts
 9 (AW) Aviation Weather
10 (WM) Weather Maps
Enter choice!
```

Fig. 10.3 *The WEATHER REPORTS menu, from which you can choose a type of forecast.*

Type **sf** or **1** to choose short-term forecasts. A prompt appears, asking you to type the name of the city and the two-letter postal abbreviation for the state, separated by commas. If you are uncertain about the spelling of a city's name, type the first few letters (four or five); if CompuServe is uncertain which city you mean, a menu of choices appears.

You use the same techniques when you choose options 2 through 4 that you use when you choose option 1. Option 5, State Summaries, on the other hand, obviously does not prompt for a city name. You must type the two-letter state abbreviation used by the U.S. Postal Service. Other options prompt you for the region in a similar way.

To get help, type **h**. (To receive help from a prompt other than the ! prompt, you must type a backslash before the command; for example, you type **\h** to get help.)

Using Classified Ads

Just as you can place ads in local newspapers, you also can place ads on CompuServe, which offers a nationwide classified ad forum. The difference between placing an ad on CompuServe and placing an ad in the newspaper, however, is that the CompuServe ad is accessed by people all over the country.

Normally, CompuServe does not permit advertising or soliciting in forums; however, CIS sets this forum aside specifically for this purpose. Ads of a sexual nature and "personals" and are not permitted, however. In addition, pasting an ad incurs a fee over and above connect time and network charges.

To access a menu that provides options for reading and submitting ads, type **go classifieds**. The Classified Ads menu, shown in figure 10.4, appears.

```
Classified Ads
 1 Browse/Read Ads
 2 Age of Ads to Read (currently ALL)
 3 Reply to an Ad
 4 Submit an Ad ($)
 5 Renew Your Ad ($)
 6 Delete Your Ad
 7 Instructions/Fees
 8 Feedback to Classified Ads Manager
Enter choice!
```

Fig. 10.4 *The Classified Ads menu.*

This menu offers the following options:

- *1 Browse/Read Ads.* This option, which enables you to read current CompuServe ads, displays a menu of categories from which you can choose.

- *2 Age of Ads to Read (currently ALL).* This option enables you to adjust the age of the ads displayed by option 1. You can restrict the display to the ads posted in the past month, for example.

- *3 Reply to an Ad.* This option enables you to compose an answer to an ad. This command is also available while using option 1 to browse and read ads.

- *4 Submit an Ad ($).* This option enables you to compose and submit an ad. Using this option incurs a surcharge, the amount of which you can discover by choosing option 7.

- *5 Renew Your Ad ($).* This option, which also incurs a surcharge, enables you to renew your ad.

- *6 Delete Your Ad.* This option enables you to delete your ad from the classifieds.

■ *7 Instructions/Fees.* This option gives you instructions on how to use the classifieds and informs you about the cost.

■ *8 Feedback to Classified Ads Manager.* This option enables you to compose a message to the Classifieds manager.

Using the CompuServe Information Manager

Much of this book is devoted to helping you use the text commands of CompuServe. If you use CIS regularly, you may notice that keeping track of the available services and their commands can be difficult. You also may notice that learning commands can be an expensive process.

If you own an IBM compatible computer or a Macintosh, help is available in the form of the *CompuServe Information Manager* (CIM). By acting as a "front end" and freeing you from the necessity of remembering <u>textual commands</u>, this ✳ program greatly simplifies using CompuServe.

This chapter is intended as an introduction and reference to CIM. The manual that accompanies the program is far more extensive. Use this chapter to help you remember how to perform CIM tasks when the manual is not available.

but you have been using menus. What is the difference? You do not explain except on page 123, and you do not expand on this here?

Configuring CompuServe Information Manager

Whether you use an IBM compatible or Macintosh computer, you must configure your version of CIM before you can use it. This section provides information and instructions to help you accomplish this task.

Configuring the Macintosh Version

After installation (check the manual that accompanies the program for installation procedures) but before you log on to CIS, you set CIM to access CompuServe by following these steps:

1. Double-click the CompuServe Information Manager icon to start it.

2. Choose the Sessions Settings command from the Special menu.

   The Sessions Setting dialog box, in which you enter the information necessary to access CompuServe, appears (see fig. 11.1).

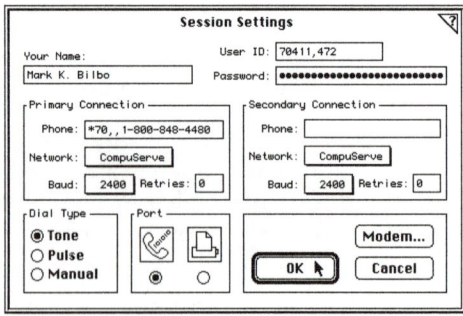

Fig. 11.1 *The Session Settings dialog box for the Mac.*

3. Type your user ID number in the User ID text box and press Tab to move to the next item.

4. Type your name in the Your Name text box and press Tab.

5. Type your password in the Password text box (the password doesn't appear; instead, you see one dot for each character) and press Tab.

6. In the Phone text box, type the phone number of the node that you use to connect with CompuServe.

   If you don't know the local access number, you can use the 800 number (1-800-848-4480) within the U.S. Then you can locate a local access number (if one exists) on-line.

   You can precede the number with various access codes. In many locations, for example, *70 cancels the Call Waiting option offered by many local phone companies (check with your phone company to see if you can use *70). The example shown in the Macintosh Session Settings dialog box illustrates how to precede a phone number with access codes. The commas, which appear after the *70 code, cause CompuServe to pause for the dial tone. One comma is usually sufficient, but you can use two or more.

   If you must dial 9 or another code to access an outside line, precede the phone number with a 9 and a comma.

7. Choose the network you are going to use from the Network pop-up menu. Choose CompuServe if you use the 800 number.

8. Choose the baud rate of your modem from the Baud pop-up menu.

9. In the Retries text box, enter a number to specify how many times the program should try to connect to CompuServe before giving up.

10. Optionally, repeat steps 6 through 9 to specify a network, phone number, and so forth for a secondary connection that you can use if the first fails entirely. If you decide not to set a secondary connection, proceed to step 11.

11. Click Tone or Pulse, depending on whether your phone line can accept TouchTone dialing or needs rotary dial pulses. Click Manual if you, rather than a modem, must dial the phone number.

12. Click the port to which your modem is connected. Although this port is normally the phone port (with the phone handset icon), it can be the printer port if your modem is connected to the printer.

13. If your modem needs special control characters, you must click the Modem button before you click OK. Your modem manual and the CIM manual can help you determine whether clicking the Modem button is necessary.

14. Click OK.

Configuring the IBM Version

To configure the IBM version, follow these steps:

1. Type **cim** at the C prompt (or other prompt, depending on the disk on which you installed CIM).

2. Press Alt+P to open the Special menu. (Alt+S opens the Services menu.)

3. Highlight the Session Settings command and press Enter. Alternatively, press **S**).

   The Sessions Settings dialog box appears (see fig. 11.2).

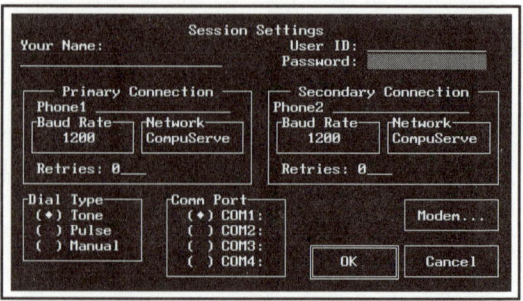

Fig. 11.2 The Session Settings dialog box for the IBM.

4. Type your name at the Your Name prompt and press Tab to move to the next prompt.

5. At the User ID prompt, type your user ID and press Tab.

6. Type your password at the Password prompt and press Tab.

7. At the Phone1 prompt in the Primary Connection section of the dialog box, type the phone number of your local access node (if you are within the U.S. and uncertain of the local access node number, type **1-800-848-4480**) and press Tab.

   You can precede the number with *70 to cancel Call Waiting (if available in your area) or 9 to access an outside line if necessary. Follow either of these with a comma before the phone number.

8. Use the up- or down-arrow key to choose the baud rate of your modem in the Baud Rate box and press Tab.

9. Indicate the number of times the program should redial the phone number before giving up (leaving this set to 0 is usually fine); press Tab.

10. Use the up- or down-arrow key to choose the network that you are using to access CompuServe; then press Tab.

11. Repeat steps 7 through 10 for the optional secondary connection that should be used if the first connection doesn't work. If you skip this step, press Tab until the insertion point reaches the Dial Type option.

12. Use the up- or down-arrow key to select the type of dialing: Tone for TouchTone phones, Pulse for rotary dial phones, or Manual if you dial the phone number yourself; then press Tab.

13. Use the up- or down-arrow key to select COM1, 2, 3, or 4, depending on which port your modem is connected to. Press Tab.

14. If your modem needs special codes (for instance, because it isn't Hayes compatible), press Enter to open the Modem Control Strings window. Enter these strings according to the information in your modem manual. Press Enter when you are finished.

15. Press Tab to highlight the OK button; then press Enter.

Logging On to CompuServe

✗ Yes it does SPECIAL TERMINAL

Neither CIM version—IBM or Macintosh—has a log on command because you log on to CompuServe automatically whenever you choose a command, such as Send Mail in Out Basket, that requires CompuServe. You do have a Disconnect command in the File menu, however. Use this command to leave CompuServe.

Navigating CompuServe   *So how have we logged on?*

Navigating through the CompuServe menus is greatly simplified by using CIM. The Macintosh version starts with an icon oriented Browse palette and moves to menus.

The IBM version, on the other hand, presents a series of menus that enable you to move easily from location to location. If you use a mouse with your IBM, you *pull down* menus in a manner similar to that of the Macintosh version. Place the mouse pointer on the menu name and press and hold the mouse button to display the menu; then move the mouse pointer down the menu while holding the mouse button. As the mouse pointer moves over commands, the commands become highlighted. When the appropriate menu command is highlighted, release the mouse button to choose the command.

If you do not have a mouse, you can do one of two things to access the menus: you can hold down the Alt key and press the first letter of the appropriate menu (Alt+F, for example, to access the File menu), or you can press the F10 key to open the first menu (File). In either case, you use the left- and right-arrow keys to move to other menus. The up- and down-arrow keys highlight the various menu commands. Press Enter to execute the highlighted command.

Using the Macintosh Version

When you first start CIM, the Browse palette appears (see fig. 11.3). The palette contains an icon for each of the main CompuServe topics. You double-click a topic that interests you. Double-clicking a topic does two things. First, if you are not logged on to CIS, double-clicking logs you on. Second, it opens a window that contains the subtopics within that topic, listed by name.

Fig. 11.3 The Browse palette.

You navigate through the menus by double-clicking the item in which you are interested. In this way, you move through the menus until you reach your destination. You can back up one or more menus by using the pop-up menu in the top part of the window.

Using the IBM Version

When you first log on, the Browse menu appears (see fig. 11.4). *How did we log on?*

```
┌──────────────── Browse ────────────────┐
│ Computer & Software Support             │
│ Special Interest Groups (Forums)        │
│ News, Weather & Sports                  │
│ Investing & Finance                     │
│ Reference Library                       │
│ Travel                                  │
│ Games                                   │
│ Shopping                                │
│ Communications                          │
│ Personal Interests & Hobbies            │
│ Professional Interests                  │
│ European Services                       │
│ Membership Support Services             │
└─────────────────────────────────────────┘
```

Fig. 11.4 *The Browse menu.*

Use the up- and down-arrow keys to highlight topics in the Browse menu. When the desired topic is highlighted, press Enter to choose it. To back up menus, press the Esc key. Each time you press this key, you back up one menu.

Using the Services Menu

The Services menu, which is common to both versions, contains commands that you use to navigate through CompuServe. These commands are explained in table 11.1.

Table 11.1 The Service Menu Commands

Command	Function
Favorite Places	Opens the Favorite Places window in which you store the forum and services that you use most frequently
Find	Opens a dialog box that enables you to type a keyword or phrase, enabling CIM to locate the forum or service relating to the keyword subject
Browse	Invokes the Browse palette
Go	Enables you to type a GO code to move to the specified forum or service
What's New	Transfers you to the What's New menu, which enables you to find CompuServe's notices of new services and other information

Command	Function
Special Events	Transfers you to the special events notices
Quotes	Moves you to the stock quote service of CompuServe
Weather	Transfers you to the weather forecast service
CB Simulator	Moves you to the CB Simulator service (an on-line "chat" service with several *channels*, each pertaining to different interest areas)

Working with CompuServe Mail

When you first log on to CompuServe using CIM, you are notified of waiting mail. If you use the IBM version, you see a box containing the word *Mail*. If you use the Macintosh version, you may see an icon of a mailbox. To read mail in the IBM version, double-click the mailbox; if you don't have a mouse, press Alt+Tab to highlight the icon, and then press Enter. To read mail in the Macintosh version, simply double-click the mailbox icon.

The Mail menu, which appears after you select the mail icon, contains other mail commands that you can use with CompuServe Mail. These commands are explained in table 11.2.

Table 11.2 The Mail Menu Commands

Command	Function
Get New Mail	Enables you to read the mail waiting for you without double-clicking the mailbox icon or using Alt+Tab as described earlier

continues

Table 11.2 Continued

Create Mail	Enables you to compose mail to be sent via CompuServe Mail; see Chapter 5, "Using CompuServe Mail" for addressing options
Send Mail in Out Basket	Sends the mail stored in your Out Basket (where CIM stores mail messages you compose when you are not logged on to CompuServe)
Send & Receive All Mail	Logs you on to Compu-Serve, sends the mail in your Out Basket, and retrieves new mail sent to you
Send File	Enables you to upload a file to be sent by Compu-Serve mail.
In Basket	Opens your In Basket and enables you to select the mail you downloaded from CompuServe
Filing Cabinet	Opens the filing cabinet and enables you to read mail stored within
Create Forum Message	Enables you to compose a message off-line to be posted to a forum
Address Book	Enables you to edit your address book

Why? How is it different?

Working with Forums

CIM is at its best when working with forums. You can perform many operations by menu (the IBM version) and by

double-clicking icons (the Macintosh version). This section is a reference to the menus and icons you are likely to encounter.

In the IBM version that uses a mouse and in the Macintosh version, you pull down the menus as described earlier. If you don't have a mouse, press F10 to access the menus; then use the left- and right-arrow keys to move from menu to menu, the up- and down-arrow keys to select a command, and the Enter key to execute the selected command.

Using the Macintosh Forum Status Window

In the Macintosh version, when you first enter a forum, the Forum Status window appears. The six icons of this window are listed in the following:

- *Waiting Messages.* If messages to you are waiting to be read, this icon is active (that is, it is not *grayed*). Double-click the icon to retrieve the messages.

- *New Notices.* Double-click this icon to read new notices posted by the SYSOPs.

- *Enter room.* This icon enables you to join a conference. You see a small word balloon over the door icon if a conference is going on.

- *Browse Messages.* This icon opens a window that lists the messages sections. You double-click the section of interest and browse the messages posted within.

- *Browse Libraries.* This icon opens a window that lists the libraries of the forum. Double-click the library of interest to see a list of library files.

- *Who's Here.* This icon opens a window that lists the other users currently present in the forum.

Using the IBM Welcome Window

When you first enter a forum with the IBM version of CIM, you are presented with the Welcome window, which indicates the last time you accessed the forum (if you have), the number of waiting messages addressed to you, and the number of members participating in conferences. Press Enter to dismiss the window.

If new notices are available, the New Notices! icon appears. If you are using a mouse, double-click the icon to read the notices; otherwise, press Alt+Tab to highlight the icon; then press Enter to read the notices.

Using CIM Menus in Forums

When you use CIM in forums, you also use CIM menus rather than the CompuServe menus. These menus are pull-down menus that you access by highlighting a menu name and then choosing a command or option from the list that appears.

Although the method of selecting menus and their options may be slightly different between the IBM and Macintosh versions of CIM, the menus themselves contain the same general commands. The following sections explain the options available in CIM menus, and special notations appear if a command or option pertains to only one version of CIM.

The Messages Menu

The Messages menu enables you to access CompuServe's message commands by pulling down a menu and choosing a command. The commands contained in the Messages menu are listed in table 11.3.

Table 11.3 Messages Menu Commands

Command	Function
Browse	Opens the Message Browse window from which you can select the section and topics of messages
Search	Enables you to search for a specific message

Command	Function
Get Waiting	(IBM only) Enables you to retrieve waiting messages (The Macintosh version has this command on the Forum Status palette.)
Get Single Msg.	Enables you to retrieve a single message
Mark Topic	(IBM only) Marks a topic to be retrieved (The Mac version uses a check box in the Message Browse window.)
Retrieve Marked	Retrieves the marked messages and stores them in your filing cabinet
Set Date	Enables you to set the date for the earliest message that will be considered new
Create Message	Opens the Compose window in which you can create a message to be posted
Send Messages	(IBM only) Enables you to review and send messages you have created
Send Messages in Out Basket	(Mac only) Enables you to send the messages stored in your Out Basket
Filing Cabinet	Enables you to access stored messages
In Basket	Opens the In Basket window and enables you to read and compose replies to retrieved messages
Address Book	Enables you to add and edit the names and addresses of CIS members stored in your address book
Notice	Enables you to read the message area notice
Description	Enables you to read the message area's description

The Libraries Menu

The Libraries menu contains the commands that enable you to access the files in the library of the forum. The menu commands are listed in table 11.4.

Table 11.4 The Libraries Menu Commands

Command	*Result*
Browse	Opens a window from which you select a library to browse
Search	Enables you to type a keyword to search for files matching the specified word
Retrieve File	Enables you to specify a file to retrieve
Retrieve Marked	Enables you to retrieve and store the files marked for retrieval to your disk (When you browse files, you click a check box to mark the files for retrieval.)
Contribute	Enables you to upload a file to the library
Notice	Enables you to read the library notice
Description	Enables you to read the description of the forum's library

The Conference Menu

The Conference menu contains commands related to the on-line conference feature of a forum. These commands are listed in table 11.5.

Table 11.5 Conference Menu Commands

Command	Result
Enter Room	Opens a window that enables you to select a conference room to enter; this window also indicates how many people are in that room
Who's Here	Opens the Who's Here window, which lists the names or user IDs of the members in the forum; click a button to see the names or user IDs of conference room members
Tracking	Enables you to set the items—who enters, who leaves, who changes locations, and so on—that are tracked in the tracking window which appears when you enter a forum
Record Incoming Text	Records the conference, using the file name you specify; stores text on disk and displays text on-screen
Set Nickname	Enables you to shorten your name
Listen	Enables you to listen to a conference but not participate, or listen to one conference while participating in another
Ignore	Enables you to block out comments from a particular member
Invite	Enables you to invite a member in the Who's Here list to a group conversation (a private conversation area others can only access if invited)
Ignore Invitations	Enables you to avoid being interrupted by blocking out invitations
Talk	Enables you to invite a member for a private (one-to-one) conversation; choose the command, then the member

continues

Table 11.5 Continued

Ignore Talks	Blocks out the talk requests of other users
Notice	Enables you to read the notice containing the forum's conference schedule
Description	Enables you to read the description of the conference area

The Special Menu

The Special menu contains several miscellaneous commands related to the forum. These commands are listed in table 11.6.

Table 11.6 Special Menu Commands

Command	Function
Notices	Enables you to select and read any of the several forum notices
Forum Options	Opens a window from which you set forum options, such as your forum name, the sections you want to view, and so on
Forum Status	Opens (or brings forward) the Forum Status window from which you choose the area—message area, library, conference, and so on—in which to work
Join Forum	Enables you to join a forum if you have not done so
Search Membership	Searches the membership database of the forum for members whose name, user ID, or interests match the entries you specify in the dialog box accessed by this command
Change Member Entry	Enables you to edit or add your own entry in the membership database

Working with Other Services

In most cases, when you enter any service, a window opens, and the familiar CIS menu appears. Choose a service from this menu; to learn about the available commands for the chosen service, refer to the appropriate sections of this book.

When you are finished using a service, click the close box of the window to return to the graphic interface of CIM.

Using Navigator

Navigator, which is a Macintosh program developed to speed access to forums on CompuServe, is intended primarily for the person who makes extensive use of CompuServe's forums. Navigator belongs to a class of *auto-pilot* programs. As the name implies, you can define actions that you want to be taken automatically by Navigator when you log on. (Other services may be accessed through a terminal mode.)

Configuring Navigator

Each time you log on to CompuServe using Navigator, you create a *session*—the time between logging on and logging off. Before you attempt to log on to CompuServe, however, you must configure the program. To configure Navigator, follow these steps:

1. Choose New from the File menu or press ⌘+N to create a new session file. The session database appears.

   The session database window is arranged in *tiles*, which are rectangles that contain the icon and name of each forum or service in the database.

2. Double-click the CompuServe Session Parameters tile. The CompuServe Session Parameters window, shown in figure 12.1, appears.

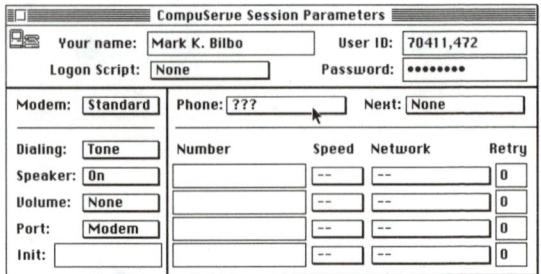

Fig. 12.1 The CompuServe Session Parameters window.

3. Type your name in the Your Name text box; then press Tab to move to the next text box.

4. Type your user ID in the User ID text box and press Tab.

5. In the Password text box, type your password and press Tab.

6. Choose the dialing type (Tone or Pulse) from the Dialing pop-up menu.

   If you use a modem that is not Hayes-compatible, check the Navigator manual and your modem manual for information about creating a dialing script.

7. Choose On, Off, or Quiet Dial from the Speaker pop-up menu (leaving this option set to On is usually acceptable).

8. Choose the desired modem speaker volume (High, Medium, Low, or None) from the Volume pop-up menu.

9. From the Port pop-up menu, choose the port (Modem or Printer) that your modem is connected to.

10. To create groups of node numbers for Navigator to use, choose the Create command from the Phone pop-up menu.

11. Type a name for this number (or group of numbers) and press Return.

12. Type the first phone number for this group. Precede the number with *70 to cancel Call Waiting if Call Waiting is available in your area. You also can precede the number with other access codes, such as 9 (often used to access an outside line). Follow the codes with a comma to enable the program to pause for a dial tone before dialing the phone number.

    (*Note:* Within the U.S., you can use 1-800-848-4480 if you are uncertain about the local node number.)

13. Choose your modem speed (or the node speed if slower) from the Speed pop-up menu.

14. Choose the network you use to access CompuServe from the Network pop-up menu.

15. Optionally, double-click the Retry field and type the number of times that you want the program to redial this phone number if the connection fails.

    To specify secondary numbers in this group in case the first fails, click the next Number field and repeat steps 12 through 14.

16. Repeat steps 10 through 15 to create other groups of numbers. Creating other groups of numbers is useful if you travel and want to predefine phone numbers for your destination.

17. Choose the number set you want to use from the Phone pop-up menu. From the Next pop-up menu, choose a secondary number to use in case the first fails. (Choosing a secondary number is optional; you can leave the Next pop-up menu set to None).

Working with CompuServe Mail

To access mail commands, double-click the CompuServe Mail System tile in the database to open a window that displays the mail commands. Initially, this window contains only the Read the Mail command; however, you can use the

Commands menu at the top of this window to choose another mail command. The available menu options are listed in table 12.1.

Table 12.1 The Commands Menu

Option	Result
Edit Messages	Opens a window that enables you to select and edit messages you wrote
Create a Message	Enables you to create a message to be mailed
Send a File	Enables you to select and address a file to be uploaded to the mail system
Delete a Command	Opens a window that lists the mail commands to be executed when you next log on (to delete a command, select it and click the Delete button)
DO NOT ENTER this Location	Prevents Navigator from entering the mail system at the next log on
Forget this Location	Removes this location from the list of locations in the Preview window so that Navigator doesn't enter the CompuServe Mail System tile until you double-click the tile in the database and enter a mail command
Read the Mail	Causes the waiting mail to be downloaded from CompuServe when you next log on so that after Navigator logs off CIS, you can read the mail and create responses to be sent in the next session

Option	Result
Summarize the Mail	Causes Navigator to give you a summary of the waiting mail but doesn't download or delete the mail
Delete after Reading	Causes downloaded (read) mail to be deleted from CompuServe so that your CIS mail box doesn't get so full that mail is rejected

Working with Forums

Navigator is geared to forum use. When you look at the database, you see that the tiles of the database contain the forum commands. To set the commands (post messages, download files, and so on), you must open the forum's tile.

Understanding a Forum's Tile

You locate a forum's commands by opening the appropriate tile. You can use one of two methods to open a tile. With the first method, you double-click the tile of the *category* that interests you (Macintosh Forums, for example) and then double-click the tile of the *forum* that interests you.

Using the second method, you choose the Find Tile command from the Search menu, type a string to be located (*Macintosh*, for example), and press Return. The first tile (if any) that contains the string you typed opens. You can choose the Find Again command from the Search menu (alternatively, press ⌘+A) to locate other tiles that contain your string.

The Forum Menu

Each forum tile contains a Forum menu. This menu contains general commands, listed in the following:

■ *DO NOT ENTER the Forum.* Choose this command if you do not want Navigator to enter the forum; previously entered commands are retained, however. Choose this command again (removing the check mark to the left of it) to enable Navigator to enter the forum.

■ *Update Section Names.* Choose this command if you want Navigator to check the section names of the forum and update the list of section names upon entry into the forum.

■ *Update My Forum Name.* Choose this command if you want Navigator to update your name when you enter the forum. By choosing the command again, you *toggle* the command off so that your name is not updated when you enter the forum.

■ *Forget this Location.* Choose this command to eliminate the forum and all commands entered from your sessions. The forum no longer appears in your session preview, and Navigator doesn't enter the forum again unless you open the forum tile and enter commands.

The Message Menu

The Message menu of the forum tiles is similar to that of the CompuServe Mail tile; for instance, messages are composed and created in the same way. Two commands specific to forums, however, are included in the Message menu. The commands of the forum Message menu are explained in table 12.2.

Table 12.2 The Message Menu

Command	Result
Edit Messages	Opens a window that enables you to select a message to edit

Command	Result
Create a Message	Opens a window that enables you to create a message to be sent in the next session
DO NOT ENTER the Message Area	Prevents Navigator from entering the message area, but retains previously entered message commands; toggle this command on or off; library commands are unaffected
Get My New Messages	Enables Navigator to automatically download all new messages addressed to you
Summarize My New Messages	Enables Navigator to tell you the message number, section, subject, and sender of new messages but doesn't download the text; use if you download entire threads and do not want to download messages directed to you twice
Get Messages by Section	Opens a window that enables you to select message commands by forum section: download all new messages in a section, acquire a summary of all new messages in a section, or ignore a section
Message Commands	Opens a window in which you place message commands; the Add button opens another window from which you choose commands to download a single message, an entire thread, messages from a particular sender, and so on

12

The Library Menu

The Library menu contains the commands that can help you locate, download, and upload files. The commands are listed in the following:

- *DO NOT ENTER the Library Area.* This command prevents Navigator from entering the library area. The library area is ignored until you choose this command again (thus removing the check mark). The Message commands are unaffected.

- *Search for Files.* This command opens a window that enables you to specify sections in which to search for files; for example, you can search a library by clicking the appropriate check box. You also can search the library automatically for new files. The Add button in this window enables you to specify keywords, file names, user IDs, and date ranges as part of your search. In addition, you can specify more than one set of criteria as you search for files.

- *Download Files.* This command enables you to specify the file name and library of files to be downloaded; in the next session, Navigator automatically downloads the files and stores them to disk.

- *Upload Files.* This command enables you to specify files to be uploaded automatically to a library.

Working with Conferences

Navigator is not well suited to conferences because the only option available is the terminal mode. The CompuServe Information Manager (CIM) is a good package to consider if you frequently use conferencing. With Navigator's strengths in forum message and library use and CIM's strengths in conferencing, together they make a good combination for the CIS user. To use Navigator for a conference, follow these steps:

1. Choose the Show Database command from the Session menu. The Database window appears.

2. Double-click the Manual Mode Tiles tile; a window displaying the several manual mode tiles appears. Click any of the manual mode tiles.

3. Click the close box of the Manual Mode window, then click the close box of the Manual Mode tiles.

4. Choose Run from the Session menu to log on to CIS.

5. Click the Append button to save your previous session information, or click OK to replace this information with the current session's information.

Navigator logs on and executes any mail or forum commands you give it and beeps when you enter the manual mode in which you can type commands and use normal CIS menus. In the manual mode, you can use the conferencing commands discussed earlier in this book.

To leave the manual mode, choose the Next Task command from the OnLine menu, which is in the Session View screen that appears whenever Navigator runs (the OnLine menu only appears when Navigator is in manual mode).

Working with Other Services

At this time, Navigator offers no special features for working with other services, such as games and weather reports. You access these services in the same manner that you access a conference—by opening a Manual Mode tile as explained in the preceding section. After you access a service, you can use the service's commands, discussed earlier in this book.

To leave the manual mode, choose the Next Task command from the OnLine menu.

Running a Navigator Session

After you enter your mail, forum message, and forum library commands, you are ready to run your session. First choose the Show Preview command from the Session menu. The Session Preview window, which shows all actions that Navigator will take in the next session, appears (see fig. 12.2).

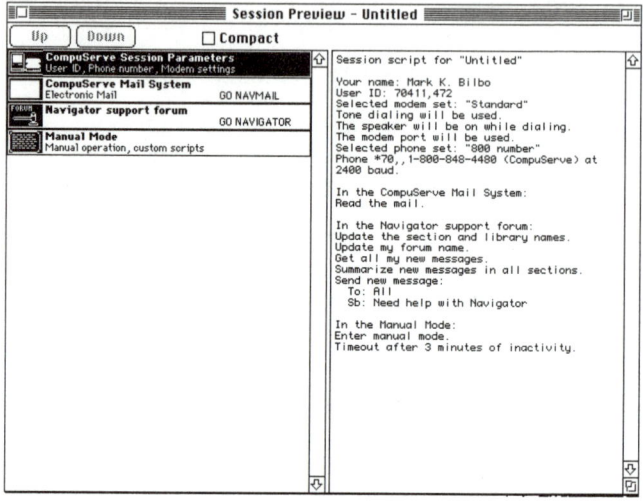

Fig. 12.2 *The Session Preview window.*

You can change the commands of the tiles listed on the left side of the screen by double-clicking the name of the tile (don't double-click the icon to the far left, however, because this disables the icon). The tile opens, and you can use the menus to edit or create messages, change or download instructions, and so on.

You disable a tile and its commands by double-clicking the icon in the far left of the tile. Enable the tile by double-clicking the icon again.

You can change the order in which the tiles are executed by clicking the tile to select it and then clicking the Up or Down button. You cannot move the Parameters tile, however. The right part of the window shows each command to be executed (refer to fig. 12.2).

This listing indicates that, when you next log on, Navigator will enter the Navigator Support forum; update the section names in its database by drawing them from the forum;

update your name in the forum; automatically download, rather than summarize, your new messages and summarize new messages in all sections; and send the new message written to All with the subject *Need help with Navigator*.

To run the session, choose the Run command from the Session menu. A notice indicating that you are about to overwrite the previous session appears. If this is your first session, click OK. If you have run a previous session, however, and want to retain messages and other material retrieved in that session, click Append. If you don't want to run the session at this time, click Cancel.

Reviewing a Navigator Session

After a session has been run, you may want to review the session to check what mail you received, what messages were posted, and so on. Choose Show Review from the Session menu. The Session Review window appears. The four buttons on this menu are explained in the following list, and the three menus—Archives, Mail, and Messages—are explained in table 12.3. (*Note:* The Messages menu is the pop-up menu above the Prior button.)

- *Reply*. When you are reading a mail or forum message, you can click this button to create a reply. Type the text of the message; Navigator enters the subject and address information.

- *Create*. To create an entirely new message, click this button to open the window in which you compose and address the message.

- *Prior*. By clicking this button, you move to the preceding message or screen.

- *Next*. By clicking this button, you move to the next message or screen.

You can use the following commands of the Messages menu to change the meaning of the Prior and Next buttons, which enable you to move by message, thread, section, location, or session:

■ *Move by Message.* This command causes the buttons to move by one message or screen at a time (the default).

■ *Move by Thread.* This command causes the buttons to move by one thread.

■ *Move by Section.* This command causes the buttons to move by section.

■ *Move by Location.* This command causes the buttons to move by location.

■ *Move by Session.* This command causes the buttons to move by session.

Table 12.3 Menus in the Session Review Window

Menu	Function
Archives	Contains a list of archive files you create with the Set Archives command of the Settings menu; you save a message or screen to the archive file by choosing the archive file's name from this menu
Mail	Contains two commands that enable you to delete messages, and record names and user IDs of people sending messages
Add Sender to ID Book	Adds to your address book the name and user ID of the people who send messages to you (look up the name and address by choosing Show ID Book from the Session menu or by clicking the Lookup button in the Message Create window)
Delete This Message	Orders the message (posted by you or addressed to you) to be deleted in the next session
Message	Contains several commands that enable you to move within the session file

Menu	*Function*
Go Next Message	Displays the next message or screen
Go Next Thread	Displays the first message of the next message thread
Go Next Section	Displays the first message of the next section
Go Next Location	Displays the first screen of the next location (which is the next forum or service you accessed during the preceding Navigator session)
Go Next Session	Displays the first screen of the next session (if you use the Append button when running sessions, you can store more than one session in your session file)
Go Prior Message	Displays the preceding message or screen
Go Prior Thread	Displays the first message of the preceding message thread
Go Prior Section	Displays the first message of the preceding section
Go Prior Location	Displays the first screen of the prior location (being the preceding forum or service you accessed)
Go Prior Session	Displays the first screen of the preceding session (if you use the Append button when running sessions, you can store more than one in your session file)

12

Using TAPCIS

TAPCIS is a program intended for IBM users of CompuServe who utilize forums extensively. Although TAPCIS is geared to forum use, it is not well suited for other aspects of CIS; however, if you find yourself using forums extensively— carrying on many conversations and posting many messages, for example—you will certainly want to have TAPCIS to speed your use and reduce costs.

Configuring TAPCIS

To configure TAPCIS, you must begin by downloading TAP.EXE, following the instructions given elsewhere in this book for downloading files.

After downloading TAP.EXE, you must expand it by typing **tap** at the C prompt. (Drive C is used throughout this discussion; however, you can substitute another drive letter if necessary.) The program expands and verifies itself.

After you download and expand the file, you are ready to set the program's parameters. These parameters, which enable TAPCIS to log on to CIS, include items—your name and user ID, for example—that you must enter before logging on to CIS with TAPCIS.

Setting Parameters

To start TAPCIS, type **tapcis** at the C prompt. The program starts and asks for your full name. Type your name and press Enter. The main TAPCIS screen appears. To set TAPCIS parameters, follow these steps:

1. Press **P** (Parameters). The parameters screen appears.

2. Set the communications port if TAPCIS has not already selected the correct one. COM1 should be displayed. If your modem is connected to a port other than COM1, press **C** until the correct port (COM1, COM2, and so on) is displayed.

   If you are using a Hayes-compatible modem, parameters I (Initialize), O (Connect), F (Fail), and R (Reset) should already be set correctly and you can skip steps 3 through 6 and proceed with step 1 of the instructions for entering parameters specific to CompuServe. If you are not using a Hayes-compatible modem, however, you must perform steps 3 through 6. You find the information for these settings in your modem manual.

3. Press **I** (Initialize), type the string your modem needs to be initialized, and press Enter.

4. Press **O** (Connect), type the string your modem sends back when a connection is made, and press Enter.

   If this string is more than four characters (Hayes modems, for example, send the word *CONNECT*), type the last four letters—**NECT**, for example. Type the characters exactly as they are sent; upper- and lowercase letters, in this instance, *do* make a difference.

5. Press **F** (Fail), type the string your modem sends back when the connection fails, and press Enter.

   This fail string setting defaults to HAYES, meaning that this string is set to catch most Hayes-compatible fail strings. Change this string, using just the last four letters, only if your modem uses a nonstandard fail report string.

6. Press **R** (Reset), type your modem reset string, and press Enter. Change this only if your modem is not Hayes-compatible.

After you set these items, you can enter the information specific to CompuServe by following these steps:

1. Press **T** (Phone Number), type the phone number of the node to which you normally connect, and press Enter.

   You can precede the phone number with codes or access numbers—*9* to access an outside line or *70* to cancel call waiting, for example. A comma should separate these special numbers and the phone number.

2. Type the baud rate of your modem (2400, for example) and press Enter.

3. To include alternate phone numbers, press **2**, **3**, **4**, **5**, or **6** to select the telephone number and baud rate to set; then repeat steps 1 and 2.

4. Press **U** (User ID) to enter your user ID.

5. Type your user ID number and press Enter.

6. Press **P** (Password) and then **Y** to confirm that you want to change the password.

7. Type your password and press Enter; then press **Y** to store the password to disk.

8. Press **S**, type the path that indicates where TAPCIS files should be stored, and press Enter.

9. Press **D**, type the path that indicates where the downloaded files should be stored, and press Enter.

To keep a monthly log of file transfers and the time you spend on CompuServe, three options are available: file transfers only, time only, and both file transfers and time. To keep a monthly log, follow these steps:

1. Press **L** (Log) one, two, or three times to set the log option. Press **L** again to change the option (pressing L moves you through the options).

2. Press **M** to open a screen that enables you to set the colors that TAPCIS uses in its window and text displays.

3. Press **N** to set the normal color; then choose a color by typing a number from 1 to 127. You use the same technique to set colors for the other options, pressing **R** to set reverse video color, **H** to set the highlight color, and so forth.

   A sample of your selection appears.

4. Press **Q** to return to the parameter screen.

5. Press **A** to set the Append the Overwrite option. Press **A** again if you prefer to accumulate messages, having each new message appended to the message file rather than having the new message overwrite existing messages. If you prefer, press **Q** to set the message file to be overwritten (losing previous messages but saving disk space).

6. Press **K** to set the outbox File Save option which determines whether your replies are retained on disk or overwritten after being sent.

7. To always save the messages you send, press **A**; to save only the mail you send, press **M**; to save none of your messages, press **N** (of course, you can always obtain your forum messages later by reading them).

8. To change your name, press **M**, type your name, and press Enter.

9. Press F7 to exit the parameters screen.

Setting CompuServe Parameters On-Line

After setting TAPCIS parameters, you must log on once to enable TAPCIS to set your CIS parameters to settings that it can use. For example, TAPCIS sets your CIS user profile to conform to the TAPCIS mode of operation.

You can use TAPCIS to set your CIS parameters automatically. Make sure your modem is hooked up and turned on; then at the main screen, press Alt+P. TAPCIS logs on and sets the appropriate parameters for you. A considerable amount of information scrolls across your screen during this process, but you do not have to take action yourself.

Setting Forums

You must set up at least one forum to use with TAPCIS to be able to log on and use CIS. After the first forum is set up, you can add forums by using the same process. To set up a forum to use with TAPCIS, follow these steps:

1. At the main screen, press **F** (Forum).

   CIS:MAIL (CompuServe Mail) should already be defined and is a good initial setting.

2. Type **A** to select CIS:MAIL.

3. To add a new forum, press F2.

4. Type the forum name (**issues forum**, for example) and press Enter.

5. Type the gateway and press Enter.

   The *gateway* is the service on which the forum exists. Although most forums reside on CIS, some forums exist on other systems, such as PC Magnet (PCM:). Essentially, the gateway code you enter here is a three-letter code that precedes the GO code so that you can get to the specified forum. If you normally enter a forum without typing a three-letter code before its GO code, enter **CIS:** as the gateway code.

6. Type the sections you want to use and press Enter.

   All is the default. If you know the numbers of the sections, you can enter them (be sure to separate the section numbers with commas); otherwise, press Enter to accept the default setting.

7. Enter **Q** (Summary) if you want the system to scan the sections and download summaries of the new messages; enter **R** (Read) if you want the system to read all new messages in the selected sections; enter **M** (Read Waiting) if you want the system to read messages waiting for you.

8. Select the forum by pressing the letter (A, B, C, and so forth) to the left of the forum name. To select CIS:MAIL (which should be in slot A), for example, press **A**. An asterisk (*) appears to the right of the selected forum. You can deselect a forum by pressing its letter again.

9. Repeat steps 3 through 8 to add more forums, if necessary.

10. Press F7 to save your changes and return to the main screen.

Even if you joined a forum earlier, you must do so again with TAPCIS in order to download the forum configuration required by TAPCIS. Do this by pressing Alt+J. TAPCIS logs on to CIS and automatically acquires the needed information.

After you complete the setup procedure, you can begin working with TAPCIS.

Working with Forums

Although working with forums is greatly speeded and simplified with TAPCIS, it may take a bit of practice to get used to how the program operates. The automated commands execute for all forums—including Mail—that you select (selected forums appear in the main screen). The following section discusses how to set the forums you want TAPCIS to enter in the current log on session.

Setting Forums to Use

Unlike Navigator, which is explained in Chapter 12, TAPCIS doesn't know that a forum exists until you tell it. To enable TAPCIS to enter a forum that you have defined but not selected (the forum name doesn't appear on the main screen), follow these steps:

1. Press **F** to make the Forum list appear.

2. Press the forum's letter (A, B, C, and so on).

3. Press F7 to save your forum choice.

Use the same steps to enable a forum not currently displayed on the main screen.

Getting and Reading New Messages

To log on to a forum and get messages waiting for you, as well as to execute the Q (Summary), R (Read), or M (Read Waiting) command you entered for the forum (refer to step 7 in "Setting Forums"), press **N** at the main screen. TAPCIS logs on, downloads messages waiting for you, and then executes the Summary, Read, or Read Waiting command you set for the forum in the selected sections.

Table 13.1 Navigating through Messages

Key/Key Combination	Result
PgUp	Display preceding message or screen
PgDn	Display next message or screen
Home	Move to first message in file
End	Move to last message in file
Shift+F6	Display next thread
Shift+F5	Move up by thread
Ctrl+F6	Display next section
Ctrl+F5	Display preceding section
F8	Display next forum
Shift+F8	Display preceding forum
Alt+F6	Display next session
Alt+F5	Display preceding session

Replying to Messages

As you read messages, you may want to reply to one. To reply to a message that you are reading, press **R** (Read) when the message is on-screen. After you read the message, you can type your reply. You also can use one of the commands listed in table 13.2 as you create a reply.

Table 13.2 Commands Used in Creating a Reply

Press	Purpose
U	Use the From address (the address of the sender) and add a new subject and section
T	Use the To address (the person receiving the message) and add a new subject and section
C	Reply to the message but post the reply in a different forum
W	Write a message with any subject and address it to anyone in any section
Tab	Forward the message by CompuServe mail
S	Save the message to the *FORUM*.SAV file (the name of the forum is substituted for *FORUM* in this name)
Ins	Enter the name of a file in which the message should be saved
A	Add the message sender or recipient to your address book
Alt+D	Order a message from or to you to be deleted in the next session

When you complete your message, press F7 to save the message so that it can be sent in the next session. Press F1 if you change your mind and want to discard the reply message.

Understanding Message Status

When you are reading messages, the upper right of the screen displays the status box. The status messages that appear are described in table 13.3.

Table 13.3 Status Messages

Status	Meaning
More	The message is too long to fit on-screen; use the up or down arrows to scroll it.
Read	You have read this message before in this session.
Saved	The message was saved to the *FORUM*.SAV file on disk.
Filed	The message was saved in a file other than the *FORUM*.SAV file.
NewFile	The message was saved in a new file.
Replied	You have replied to the message at least once.
Fwded	You have forwarded the message.
Printed	You have printed the message.
DelCIS	The message will be deleted in the next session.
New	The message is from the most recent session.
Old	The message is from a prior session.

Working with the Library Area

You can use TAPCIS to search for and download files. You use the same concepts discussed in Chapter 4, "Using Forums," which covers forum libraries, but in an automated way; in other words, the same commands are used, but TAPCIS issues them automatically.

Searching for Files

To search for a file, follow these steps:

1. Press **L** at the main screen.

2. Press the number of the forum you want to use.

3. If you know the name of the file, type it and press Enter; otherwise, press Enter without entering a file name.

4. Type the keyword or keywords (separated by commas) for which you want to search and press Enter. To match all keywords, press Enter without entering keywords.

5. Type the maximum age of the file(s) you want to find.

   Enter the age range according to the following examples:

Age	Meaning
30	Thirty or fewer days since upload
30-	Thirty or more days since upload
30-60	Uploaded in the past thirty to sixty days

   To match all files regardless of when they were uploaded, press Enter without entering an age.

6. Type **L** for long descriptions of the files (best) or **S** for short descriptions; then press Enter.

7. Type the library or libraries (separated by commas) to be searched and then press Enter. Type **all** to search all libraries in the forum.

8. Press **Y** if you want to enter more searches (with different keywords, perhaps) or press Enter to quit entering searches.

9. After entering your search criteria, press **N** at the main screen to initiate the log on and the library search. Alternatively, you can perform other operations (replying to messages, for example) before going on-line.

Creating a Catalog and Downloading Files

After you acquire the list of files from a library search, press **C** at the main screen and then enter the number of the forum to create a catalog of files.

The listing of the first file that matches your criteria is displayed. To download this file in your next session, press **D**. To view the next file entry, press PgDn or Enter. By pressing PgUp, you can display the preceding file entry. When you are finished viewing files and choosing downloads, press Esc to return to the main screen.

Table 13.4 describes the commands you can use when you are working with your catalog of files.

Table 13.4 Catalog Commands

Command	Function
1	Display first file in catalog (rather than first file of most recent download)
3	Display last session
9	Display last file
?	Show list of libraries
Alt+F5	Display files from preceding session
Alt+F6	Display files from next session
B	Display preceding file
D	Download file on-screen
Enter	Display next file
F	Search for string within catalog
F2	Search for string within catalog
N	Go to next match of string
PgDn	Display next file
PgUp	Display preceding file
Space	Display next file

Uploading a File

Uploading a file enables you to contribute files to forum libraries. You must be on-line. Use the Interactive command by pressing **I**; then enter the number of the forum you want to log on to. You will be in terminal mode. To upload a file, follow these steps:

1. Type **lib** to enter the library area.

2. Type the number of the library to which you want to upload and press Enter.

3. Press PgUp to upload a file.

4. When prompted for the file name for your computer, enter the full path name.

Working with Conferences

To participate in a conference, you need to use the Interactive mode of TAPCIS. Type **I** at the main screen and type the number of the forum you want to enter; then do the following:

1. Type **co** *n*, where *n* is the number of the conference room you want to use and press Enter. If you do not know the number, type only **co** and press Enter.

   A menu of available conference rooms appears, followed by the number of people using that room in parentheses.

2. Type the number of the appropriate conference room and press Enter.

3. Press Ctrl+X to enter conference mode. Your screen splits so that you can read the comments of others as you type your own at the bottom of the screen. You press Enter to separate your messages into more than one line.

4. To send your comment, press Enter twice.

Table 13.5 describes the commands you can use in conference mode.

Table 13.5 Conference Mode Commands

Command	Function
Ctrl+U	Erase all lines
Ctrl+X	Return to terminal mode
Ctrl+Y	Erase line
Enter	New line
Enter, Enter	Send lines

13

Working with CompuServe Mail

In TAPCIS, CompuServe Mail is treated as another forum, though without the usual section headings. You send, receive, and reply to mail the same way you perform these tasks with forum messages.

Make sure that you have CIS:MAIL selected as one of your forums. To do so, press **F** at the main screen. If no asterisk is present to the right of the CIS:MAIL line (which should be line A), press the letter that appears to the left of the CIS:MAIL line. Then press F7.

Use the same commands as outlined for working with forums to create, read, and reply to mail messages.

Working with Other Services

Other services require that you enter terminal mode. Press **I** at the main screen and then type the forum number (any forum will do) After you log on, you can enter the service's GO code. The normal CIS commands for the services discussed throughout this book apply; TAPCIS acts as your terminal package but offers only one option to work with other services.

Press PgDn to capture text to disk as you work with other services.

A P P E N D I X
A

EDIT Command Summary

The EDIT editor is an alternative to the LINEDIT editor, which is the default for forums and the CompuServe Mail system. You can choose EDIT by using the Options (Opt) command in the forum or by setting your user profile to use EDIT.

EDIT can be initially difficult to use because the commands are hard to remember and it doesn't use menus; however, many users prefer EDIT to LINEDIT. This appendix summarizes the EDIT commands.

Keep in mind that EDIT operates not by line numbers but by positioning a pointer to indicate the current line. Commands operate on the current line.

Command	Meaning
/A/*text*	Append text to current line
/B	Move pointer to last line of text
/C/*old*/*new*	Replace *old* text with *new* text in the current line
/D*n*	Delete *n* lines, starting from the current line and moving down
/Exit	Leave EDIT
/Help	Display help screens

Command	Meaning
/L/*text*	Locate text and move pointer to line containing the specified text.
/N*n*	Move pointer down (positive number) or up (negative number) lines
/P*n*	Display *n* lines, starting with the current line
/Type	Display all lines

B

Navigation Command Summary

You use Navigation commands, which apply to all Compu-Serve menus, to move around in CompuServe. Although these commands apply to the CompuServe menus, they do not apply to services such as Shopper's Advantage, which is actually a separate system.

You use Navigation commands at any exclamation mark (!) prompt. For prompts other than !, precede the command with a slash (/).

Command	Meaning
?	Display help text
B	Move back one screen
F	Display next screen
GO *page*	Go to the specified page (GO Issues, for example)
H	Display help text
M	Return to preceding menu
N	Display next item on menu
P	Display preceding item on menu
R	Resend current page (use to redisplay a page that was scrambled by line noise, for example)

Command	Meaning
S*n*	Display menu item *n* without stopping between pages
T	Return to TOP menu
Off	Log off CompuServe

Control Key Command Summary

You use the Control key commands to control the flow of information to your computer. Most users of IBM or IBM-compatible systems should use the Control key (Ctrl) to execute these commands; most Macintosh users, on the other hand, should use the Command key (⌘). If you are not sure which key to use, check with the manual that comes with your communications package.

To use these commands, press and hold the Ctrl key (or the ⌘ key) as you press the other letter. For example, to cancel the current CIS operation, you hold the Ctrl key while you press C.

Command	Meaning
Ctrl+C	Cancel the current operation
Ctrl+H	Delete the letter to the left of the cursor
Ctrl+O	Cancel the current information being sent to your computer and skip the remaining information
Ctrl+S	Pause the information being sent to your computer
Ctrl+Q	Resume sending the information paused by a Ctrl+S command

Command	Meaning
Ctrl+U	Erase the last line typed before Enter is pressed
Ctrl+V	Redisplay the last line typed before Enter is pressed

The last two commands (Ctrl+U and Ctrl+V) are useful when, in conference situations, your typing is accidentally overwritten by the comments of others.

CompuServe Services

The following is an alphabetical listing of the services and forums currently offered by CompuServe and the GO code that you use to access the service or forum. To access the ABC Worldwide Hotel Guide, you type **go abc**, for example.

Service/Forum	GO Code
ABC Worldwide Hotel Guide	ABC
ACIUS Forum	ACIUS
AI EXPERT Forum	AIEXPERT
AP Sports($)	SPORTS
APPC Info Exchange Forum	APPCFORUM
ASP/Shareware Forum	ASPFORUM
AT&T Toll-Free 800 Directory(FREE)	ATT
Academic American Encycl.	ENCYCLOPEDIA
Access Phone Numbers(FREE)	PHONE
Access Technology Forum	ACCTECH
Adobe Forum	ADOBE
Advantage Communications(FREE)	AD
Adventures in Travel	AIT
Air France(FREE)	AF
Air Traffic Controller	ATCONTROL

Service/Forum	GO Code
Alamo Rent-A-Car(FREE)	AL
Aldus Customer Service Forum	ALDSVC
Aldus Display	ALDUS
Aldus/Silicon Beach Forum	SBSALDFORUM
American Express(FREE)	AE
Americana Clothing(FREE)	AC
Amiga Arts Forum	AMIGAARTS
Amiga File Finder	AMGFF
Amiga Tech Forum	AMIGATECH
Amiga User's Forum	AMIGAUSER
Amiga Vendor Forum	AMIGAVENDOR
Apparel Concepts for Men(FREE)	AP
Apple II Prog. Forum	APPROG
Apple II Users Forum	APPUSER
Apple II Vendor Forum	APIIVEN
Apple News Clips($)	APPLENEWS
Aquaria/Fish Forum	FISHNET
Art Gallery Forum	ARTGALLERY
Ashton-Tate App. Forum	ATAPP
Ashton-Tate Dev. Registry	ADR
Ashton-Tate Supp. Library	ASHTON
Ashton-Tate dBASE Forum	DBASE
Ask3Com	THREECOM
Ask3Com Forum	ASKFORUM
Associated Press($)	ENS
Associated Press Online	APV
Astrological Charting	ASTROLOGY
Astronomy Forum	ASTROFORUM
Atari 8-Bit Forum	ATARI8
Atari File Finder	ATARIFF
Atari Portfolio Forum	APORTFOLIO
Atari ST Arts Forum	ATARIARTS
Atari ST Prod. Forum	ATARIPRO

Service/Forum	GO Code
Atari Users Network	ATARINET
Atari Vendor Forum	ATARIVEN
Audio Engineering Society	AESNET
AutoQuot-R(FREE)	AQ
AutoVantage OnLine(FREE)	ATV
Autodesk AutoCAD Forum	ACAD
Autodesk Retail Products Forum	ARETAIL
Autodesk Software Forum	ASOFT
Automobile Forum	CARS
Automobile Info Center(FREE)	AI
Automotive Information	AUTO
Aviation Forum (AVSIG)	AVSIG
Aviation Menu	AVIATION
Aviation Safety Institute	ASI
BASIS International Forum	BASIS
Bacchus Wine Forum	WINEFORUM
Banyan Forum	BANFORUM
Banyan Systems Inc.	BANYAN
Barnes & Nobles Books(FREE)	BN
Berkshire Record Outlet(FREE)	RO
Billing Assistance(FREE)	QABILL
Billing Information(FREE)	BILLING
Biorhythms	BIORHYTHM
Biz*File($)	BIZFILE
BlackDragon	BLACKDRAGON
Blyth Forum	BLYTH
Boat Xpress(FREE)	BX
Bonds Listing($)	BONDS
Book Review Digest($)	BOOKREVIEW
Books in Print($)	BOOKS
Borland Appl. Forum	BORAPP
Borland International	BORLAND
Borland Products Forum	BORDB

Service/Forum	GO Code
Borland Prog. Forum A	BPROGA
Borland Prog. Forum B	BPROGB
Bose Express Music(FREE)	BEM
Boston Computer Exchange(FREE)	BCE
Boyd's Office Supplies(FREE)	BOYDS
Breton Harbor Basket Co.(FREE)	BH
British Legends	LEGENDS
Broadcast Pro Forum	BPFORUM
Brøderbund Software(FREE)	BB
Brooks Brothers(FREE)	BR
Buick Magazine(FREE)	BUICK
Business Database Plus($)	BUSDB
Business Dateline($)	BUSDATE
Business Demographics($)	BUSDEM
Business Incorp. Guide(FREE)	INC
CADKEY Forum	CADKEY
CAE & CADD/CAM Vendor Forum	CADDVEN
CASE DCI Forum	CASEFORUM
CB Club	CBCLUB
CB Forum	CBFORUM
CB Handle	HANDLE
CB Profiles	CBPROFILES
CB Simulator	CB
CB Society	CUPCAKE
CCML AIDS Articles($)	AIDSNEWS
CDA Computer Sales(FREE)	CDA
CDROM Forum	CDROM
CENDATA	CENDATA
CIM Support Forum(FREE)	CIMSUPPORT
CP/M Users Group Forum	CPMFORUM
Cabletron System, Inc.	CTRON
Calculate Net Worth	FINTOL
Cancer Forum	CANCER

Service/Forum	GO Code
Canon Support Forum	CANON
CastleQuest	CQUEST
Central Point Forum	CENTRAL
Change Terminal Type(FREE)	TERMINAL
Change Your Password(FREE)	PASSWORD
CheckFree(FREE)	CF
Chef's Catalog(FREE)	CHEFS
Chess Forum	CHESSFORUM
Citizens Band Simulator	CB
Classic Adventure	CLADVENT
Classic Quotes	TMC-45
Classifieds	CLASSIFIEDS
Client Server Computing Forum	MSNETWORKS
Coffee Anyone???(FREE)	COF
Coin/Stamp Collect. Forum	COLLECT
Color Computer Forum	COCO
Comics/Animation Forum	COMIC
Command Summary(FREE)	COMMAND
Commerce Business Daily($)	COMBUS
Commodities	COMMODITIES
Commodity Pricing($)	CPRICE
Commodity Symbol Lookup	CSYMBOL
Commodore Applications Forum	CBMAPP
Commodore Arts/Games Forum	CBMART
Commodore Newsletter	CBMNEWS
Commodore Service Forum	CBMSERVICE
Commodore Users Network	CBMNET
Compact Disc Club(FREE)	CD
Company Analyzer($)	ANALYZER
Company Screening($EW)	COSCREEN
Compendex Engineer Index($)	COMPENDEX
CompuBooks(FREE)	CBK
CompuServe Copyright(FREE)	RULES
CompuServe Europe	EUROPE

Service/Forum	GO Code
CompuServe Index(FREE)	INDEX
CompuServe Mail	MAIL
CompuServe Mail Help(FREE)	MAILHELP
CompuServe Mail Hub	MHSADMIN
CompuServe Navigator	NAVIGATOR
CompuServe Rates(FREE)	RATES
CompuServe Software	CISSOFT
CompuServe Subject Index(FREE)	TOPIC
CompuServe Tour(FREE)	TOUR
Computer Art Forum	COMART
Computer Club Forum	CLUB
Computer Consult. Forum	CONSULT
Computer Database Plus($)	COMPDB
Computer Directory($)	COMPDIR
Computer Express(FREE)	CE
Computer Language Forum	CLMFORUM
Computer Library	COMPLIB
Computer Sciences Corp.(FREE)	CSCNET
Computer Shopper(FREE)	CS
Computer Training Forum	DPTRAIN
Computer Virus Help Forum	VIRUSFORUM
Computing Tutorials	PCS-121
Consumer Elect. Forum	CEFORUM
Consumer Reports	CONSUMER
Consumer Reports Auto.	CRAUTO
Contact Lens Supply(FREE)	CL
Cooks Online Forum	COOKS
Corporate Affiliations($)	AFFILIATIONS
Crafts Forum	CRAFTS
Create-A-Book(FREE)	CK
Creative Solutions/Forth Forum	FORTH
Crosstalk Forum	XTALK
Current Day Quotes($)	QQUOTE
Current Market Snapshot	SNAPSHOT

Service/Forum	GO Code
DATASTORM Forum	DATASTORM
DEC PC Forum	DECPC
DEC Users Network	DECUNET
DECPCI Forum	DECPCI
DISCLOSURE II($E)	DISCLOSURE
DTP Vendors Forum	DTPVENDOR
Dalco Computer Electronics(FREE)	DA
Data Access Corp. Forum	DACCESS
Data Access Corporation	DAC
Data Based Advisor(FREE)	DB
Data Based Advisor Forum	DBADVISOR
Data-Process. Newsletter($)	DPNEWS
DataPac Instructions(FREE)	LOG-41
Department of State	STATE
Desktop Publishing Forum	DTPFORUM
Desktop/Electronic Publ.	DTP
Diabetes Forum	DIABETES
Digital Research Forum	DRFORUM
Digitalk Forum	DIGITALK
Direct Micro(FREE)	DM
Disabilities Forum	DISABILITIES
Discount Shopping, Inc.(FREE)	DSI
Dissertation Abstracts($)	DISSERTATION
Dividends and Splits($)	DIVIDENDS
Dow Jones & Co(FREE)	DJ
Download Pricing Data	IQINT
Dr. Dobb's Forum	DDJFORUM
Dreyfus Corporation(FREE)	DR
Dun's Canadian Mkt. Ident($)	DBCAN
Dun's Elect Business Dir($)	DYP
Dun's Market Identifiers($)	DMI
EAASY SABRE	SABRE
EAASY SABRE (CIM)	SABRECIM
EETnet	EETNET

Service/Forum	GO Code
EMI Aviation Services($)	EMI
ERIC - Education Research($)	ERIC
Education Forum	EDFORUM
Educational Advisory	EA
Educational Res. Forum	EDRESEARCH
Electronic Convention Ctr	CONVENTION
Electronic Gamer(tm)	EGAMER
Engineering Automation Forum	LEAP
Enhanced Adventure	ENADVENT
Epson Forum	EPSON
European Access Numbers	EUROPHONES
European Company Library	EUROLIB
European Logon(FREE)	EUROLOGON
Examine Detailed Issue($)	EXAMINE
Executive News Service($)	ENS
Executive Option Upgrade(FREE)	EXECUTIVE
Executive Stamper(FREE)	EX
FCC Members of Congress	FCC
Fancy Food & Specialty Gift(FREE)	FF
Fantasy/Roll-Playing Adv.	ADVENT
Feedback to CompuServe(FREE)	FEEDBACK
Figi's(FREE)	FG
Financial Documentation	FINHLP
Financial File Transfer	FILTRN
Financial File/MQUOTE II	MQUOTE
Financial Forecasts	EARNINGS
Financial Forums	FINFORUM
Financial Interfaces	INTERFACES
Financial Surcharge List	MMM-23
Flight Simulator Forum	FSFORUM
Florida Forum	FLORIDA
Florida Fruit Shippers(FREE)	FFS
Flower Stop(FREE)	FS
Ford Motor Company(FREE)	FORD

Service/Forum	GO Code
Foreign Language Forum	FLEFO
Forum Conference Schedule	OLT-120
Forum Help Area(FREE)	QAFORUM
Forums	FORUMS
Fox Software Forum	FOXFORUM
Game Forums and News	GAMECON
Game Publisher's Forum	GAMPUB
Gamers Forum	GAMERS
Gardening Forum	GARDENING
Garrett Wade Woodworking(FREE)	GW
Genealogy Forum	ROOTS
German Company Library	GERLIB
Gimmee Jimmy's Cookies(FREE)	GIM
Good Earth Forum	GOODEARTH
Government Publications	GPO
Graphics Corner Forum	CORNER
Graphics File Finder	GRAPHFF
Graphics Forums	GRAPHICS
Graphics Support Forum	GRAPHSUPPORT
Graphics Vendor Forum	GRAPHVEN
H&R Block(FREE)	HRB
HP Peripherals Forum	HPPER
HP Systems Forum	HPSYS
HSX Adult Forum	HSX200
HSX Open Forum	HSX100
Hammacher Schlemmer(FREE)	HS
Hamnet Forum	HAMNET
Handicapped User's Data	HANDICAPPED
Hangman	HANGMAN
Hardware Forums	HARDWARE
Hawaii General Store(FREE)	HAWAII
Hayes	HAYES
Hayes Forum	HAYFORUM
Health & Fitness Forum	GOODHEALTH

Service/Forum	GO Code
Health Database Plus($)	HLTDB
Health/Fitness	FITNESS
HealthNet	HNT
Hollywood Hotline	HOLLYWOOD
Home Tech Depot(FREE)	DEPOT
Human Sexuality Databank	HUMAN
IBES Earnings Est Rpts($E)	IBES
IBM Applications Forum	IBMAPP
IBM Bulletin Board Forum	IBMBBS
IBM Communications Forum	IBMCOM
IBM Desktop Soft. Forum	IBMDESK
IBM European Users Forum	IBMEUROPE
IBM File Finder	IBMFF
IBM Hardware Forum	IBMHW
IBM New Users Forum	IBMNEW
IBM OS/2 Forum	IBMOS2
IBM Programming Forum	IBMPRO
IBM Special Needs Forum	IBMSPEC
IBM Systems/Util. Forum	IBMSYS
IBM Users Network	BMNET
IQuest($)	IQUEST
IRug Forum	REALTIME
Incue Online	INCUE
InfoWorld Online Reviews	INFOWORLD
Information USA	INFOUSA
Int'l Access Info(FREE)	INTERNATIONAL
Int'l Dun's Mkt Identifier($)	DBINT
Int'l Entrepreneurs Forum	USEN
Intel Corporation	INTEL
Intelligence Test	TMC-101
Introduction to Graphics	PIC
InvesText($)	INVTEXT
Investors Forum	INVFORUM
Island of Kesmai	ISLAND

Service/Forum	GO Code
Issue Pricing Interface($)	MQINT
Issues Forum	ISSUESFORUM
JCPenney(FREE)	JCPENNEY
Javelin/EXPRESS Forum	IRIFORUM
Journalism Forum	JFORUM
K&B Camera Center(FREE)	KB
LDC Spreadsheets Forum	LOTUSA
LDC Word Processing Forum	LOTUSWP
LDC Words & Pixels Forum	LOTUSB
LDOS/TRSDOS6 Users Forum	LDOS
LOGO Forum	LOGOFORUM
Lan Technology Forum	LANTECH
Legal Forum	LAWSIG
Legal Research Center($)	LEGALRC
Literary Forum	LITFORUM
Logitech Forum	LOGITECH
Logoff Instructions(FREE)	OQA-1330
Logon Assistance(FREE)	QALOGON
Logon Instructions(FREE)	LOGON
Lotus Technical Library	LOTUSTECH
MECA Software Forum	MECA
MIDI Vendor Forum	MIDIVENDOR
MIDI/Music Forum	MIDIFORUM
MMS International	MMS
MMS/Daily Comment($)	DC
MMS/Fedwatch Newsletter($)	FW
MQDATA($)	MQDATA
MS Applications Forum	MSAPP
MS DOS 5.0 Forum	MSDOS
MS Operating Sys/Dev Forum	MSOPSYS
MS Software Library	MSL
MS Windows Advanced Forum	WINADV
MS Windows SDK Forum	WINSDK
MTM Challenge Board	MTMCHALLENGE

Service/Forum	GO Code
Mac A Vendor Forum	MACAVEN
Mac Applications Forum	MACAP
Mac B Vendor Forum	MACBVEN
Mac C Vendor Forum	MACCVEN
Mac CIM Support Forum(FREE)	MCIMSUP
Mac Communications Forum	MACCOMM
Mac Community/Club Forum	MACCLUB
Mac Developers Forum	MACDEV
Mac Entertainment Forum	MACFUN
Mac Hypertext Forum	MACHYPER
Mac New Users Help Forum	MACNEW
MacUser	MACUSER
MacUser (Subscriptions)(FREE)	MC
MacWAREHOUSE(FREE)	MW
MacWEEK	MACWEEK
Macintosh File Finder	MACFF
Macintosh Forums	MACINTOSH
Macintosh System 7.0 Forum	MACSEVEN
Macintosh Systems Forum	MACSYS
Magazine Database Plus($)	MAGDB
Magill's Survey of Cinema($W)	MAGILL
Market Highlights($)	MARKET
Market/Ind. Index Lookup(FREE)	INDICATORS
Market/Mgt Research Cent.($)	MKTGRC
Markt & Technik Deutschland	MUTFORUM
Marquis Who's Who($)	BIOGRAPHY
MaryMac Industries, Inc.(FREE)	MM
Max Ule's Tickerscreen	TKR
McGraw-Hill Book Company(FREE)	MH
Media Newsletters($)	MEDIANEWS
Medsig Forum	MEDSIG
MegaWars I	MEGA1
MegaWars III	MEGA3
Member Assistance(FREE)	HELP

Service/Forum	GO Code
Member Directory(FREE)	DIRECTORY
Member Recommendation(FREE)	FRIEND
Mensa Forum	MENSA
Mentor Technologies(FREE)	MENTOR
MicroWare Online Support	MICROWARE
MicroWarehouse(FREE)	MCW
Microsoft BASIC Forum	MSBASIC
Microsoft Central Europe Forum	MSCE
Microsoft Connection	MICROSOFT
Microsoft Excel Forum	MSEXCEL
Microsoft Knowledge Base	MSKB
Microsoft Languages Forum	MSLANG
Microsoft WIN32 Forum	MSWIN32
Military Forum	MILITARY
Miltrobe Electronics(FREE)	MI
Mission Control Software(FREE)	MCS
Model Aviation Forum	MODELNET
Modem Games Forum	MODEMGAMES
Modem/Modem Game Support	MTMGAMES
Money Mag. Fin'l Info	MONEYMAG
Money Magazine Online	MFO-11
Money's Financial Market(FREE)	MFM
Monthly Charges(FREE)	CHARGES
Mortgage Calculator	HOM-17
Motor Sports Forum	RACING
Movie Reviews	MOVIES
Multi Issue Price History($)	SHEET
Multi-Player Games Forum	MPGAMES
Multimedia Forum	MULTIMEDIA
Multimedia Vendor Forum	MULTIVEN
Multiple Zones(FREE)	MZ
Museum of Fine Arts-Bost(FREE)	FA
Music Alley Online(FREE)	MAO
NAIC Invest. Ed. Forum	NAIC

Service/Forum	GO Code
NCAA Collegiate Sports Network	NCAA
NTIS - Gov't Sponsored($)	NTIS
NWS Aviation Weather	AWX
Nantucket	NANTUCKET
Nantucket Forum	NANFORUM
Nantucket GMBH Forum	NANGMBH
Narada Productions(FREE)	NARADA
Nat. Computer Security Assoc.	NCSA
NeXT Forum	NEXTFORUM
Neighborhood Demographics($)	NEIGHBOR
Network Access Info(FREE)	NETWORK
New Age Forum	NEWAGE
New Car Showroom($)	NEWCAR
New England Business Services	NEBS
News-A-Tron($W)	NAT
NewsGrid	NEWSGRID
NewsNet(FREE)	NN
Newspaper Library($)	NEWSLIB
Nissan(FREE)	NISSAN
Node Abbreviations(FREE)	NODES
Northwest Naturally(FREE)	NW
Novell Compatibility	NOV-61
Novell Forum A	NOVA
Novell Forum B	NOVB
Novell Forum C	NOVC
Novell Library Forum	NOVLIB
Novell NetWare 2.X Forum	NETW2X
Novell NetWare 3.X Forum	NETW3X
Novell NetWire	NOVELL
Novell Tech Bullet. Dbase	NTB
OS9 Forum	OS9
OTC NewsAlert($)	ENS
Official Airline Guide EE($)	OAG
Official Airline Guides(FREE)	OA

Service/Forum	GO Code
Olympic News Clips	OLYMPICS
Omaha Steaks Intl.(FREE)	OS
Online Inquiry	OLI
Online Rates	RATES
Online Today Forum	ONLINE
Options Profile($W)	OPRICE
Oracle Forum	ORACLE
Order From CompuServe(FREE)	ORDER
Outdoor Forum	OUTDOORFORUM
Outdoors News Clips($)	OUTNEWS
Overview of IBMNET	OVERVIEW
PC Catalog(FREE)	PCA
PC Computing	PCCOMP
PC Computing(Subscribe)(FREE)	PCC
PC Contact Forum	PCCONTACT
PC MagNet	PCMAGNET
PC Magazine(Subscribe)(FREE)	PM
PC Plus Online	PCPLUS
PC Publications(FREE)	PCB
PC Sources(Subscribe)	PC
PC Vendor A Forum	PCVENA
PC Vendor B Forum	PCVENB
PC Vendor C Forum	PCVENC
PC Vendor D Forum	PCVEND
PC Vendor E Forum	PCVENE
PC Week Extra!	PCWEEK
PDP-11 Forum	PDP11
PR and Marketing Forum	PRSIG
Palmtop Forum	PALMTOP
PaperChase-MEDLINE($)	PAPERCHASE
Parlor and Trivia Games	TTGAMES
Parsons Technology	PA
Participate	PARTI

Service/Forum	GO Code
Patent Research Center($)	PATENT
Paul Fredrick Shirts(FREE)	PFS
Penny Wise Office Supply(FREE)	PW
Pepperidge Farm(FREE)	PF
Personal Computing	COMPUTERS
Personal File Area	FILES
Personal Menu	MENU
Personality Profile	TMC-90
PetWorks(FREE)	PT
Peterson College Database	PETERSONS
Peterson's Connexion(FREE)	PX
Pets/Animal Forum	PETS
Phone*File($)	PHONEFILE
Photography Forum	PHOTOFORUM
Physicians Data Query($)	PDQ
Play-By-Mail Games Forum	PBMGAMES
Portable Prog. Forum	CODEPORT
Portfolio Valuation($)	PORT
Practical Periph. Forum	PPIFORUM
Practice Forum(FREE)	PRACTICE
Price Motor Cars(FREE)	PRC
Price/Vol Graph($)	TREND
Pricing Statistics	PRISTATS
PsychINFO Abstracts($)	PSYCINFO
Publishers Clearing House(FREE)	PUB
Push Pedal Pull(FREE)	PPP
Question & Answer(FREE)	QUESTIONS
Quick Picture Forum	QPICS
Quick Reference List(FREE)	QUICK
Quick Way Brokerage($)	QWK
RUSH LIMBAUGH	GGG-118
Rare Disease Database	NORD
RateGram Fed Insured CDs(W)	RATEGRAM

Service/Forum	GO Code
Rehabilitation Database	REHAB
Religion Forum	RELIGION
Rent Mother Nature(FREE)	RM
Return Analysis($E)	RETURN
Reuters Financial Report($)	ENS
Revelation Tech Forum	REVELATION
Robertson Electronics(FREE)	RE
Rocknet Forum	ROCKNET
Roger Ebert's Movie Reviews	EBERT
Role-Playing Games Forum	RPGAMES
S&P Online($)	S&P
SAFEWARE Computer Insure(FREE)	SAF
SHOPPERS ADVANTAGE Club(FREE)	SAC
SHOWBIZ Quiz	SBQ
SNIPER!	SNIPER
SOFTEX (sm) Software Cat.	SOFTEX
SPC Forum	SPCFORUM
STAGEII	STAGEII
SUPERSITE Demographics($E)	SUPERSITE
SYM/Norton Utility Forum	NORUTL
Safetynet Forum	SAFETYNET
Sailing Forum	SAILING
Science Fiction Forum	SCI-FI
Science Trivia Quiz	SCITRIVIA
Science/Math Ed. Forum	SCIENCE
Scuba Forum	DIVING
Sears(FREE)	SEARS
Securities Screening($E)	SCREEN
Securities Symbols Lookup	SYMBOLS
Shareware Depot(FREE)	SD
Sharon Luggage and Gifts(FREE)	SL
Shop-at-home	SHOPPING
Short Sizes Inc.(FREE)	SS

Service/Forum	GO Code
ShowBiz Forum	SHOWBIZ
Sierra Online(FREE)	SI
Single Issue Price Hist.($)	PRICES
Small Computer Book Club(FREE)	BK
Soap Opera Summaries($)	SOAPS
Society of Broadcast Eng.	SBENET
Softdisk Publishing(FREE)	SP
Software Discounters(FREE)	SDI
Software Excitement(FREE)	SE
Software Forums	SOFTWARE
Software Pub. Asst. Forum	SPAFORUM
Software Publisher Online	SPC
Sounds & Video Online(FREE)	RD
Soviet Crisis Forum	USSRFORUM
Space/Astronomy Forum	SPACE
Spear, Rees & Company($)	SPEAR
Specials/Contests Menu	SPECIAL
Spinnaker Software Forum	SPINNAKER
Sports Forum	FANS
Standard Indus. Class.	SICCODE
Standard Microsystems Forum	SMC
Start Online	START
State Capitol Quiz	TMC-44
State-County Demographics($)	DEMOGRAPHICS
Stationary Center(FREE)	SC
Students' Forum	STUFO
Sunglasses/Shavers & More(FREE)	SN
Symantec Forum	SYMFORUM
TAPCIS Forum	TAPCIS
TBS Network Earth Forum	EARTH
TICFIL	TICFIL
TRW Bus. Credit Reports($)	TRWREPORT
TRW Credentials(FREE)	CRE

Service/Forum	GO Code
TSR Games Shoppe(FREE)	TSR
TV Transcripts($)	TRANSCRIPTS
TYMNET Instructions(FREE)	LOG-11
Tall Tails(FREE)	TT
Tandy Model 100 Forum	M100SIG
Tandy Newsletter	TANDY
Tandy Professional Forum	TRS80PRO
Tax Hotline	THL
Telecom Issues Forum	TELECOM
Telenet Instructions(FREE)	LOG-20
Texas Instruments Forum	TIFORUM
Texas Instruments News	TINEWS
The Business Wire	TBW
The Catalog Store(FREE)	CATALOGS
The Computer Store(FREE)	TCS
The Court Pharmacy(FREE)	RX
The Disney Catalog(FREE)	DISNEY
The Electronic MALL(FREE)	MALL
The Focus Connection	FOCUS
The Heath Company(FREE)	HEATH
The Intel Forum	INTELFORUM
The Laser's Edge(FREE)	LE
The Multiple Choice	MULTIPLE
The Programmers Shop(FREE)	PS
The Rodeo Mile(FREE)	ROD
The Tandy Users Network	TANDYNET
The Whiz Quiz	WHIZ
The World of Lotus	LOTUS
Thomas Register Online($)	THOMAS
Ticker/Symbol Lookup	LOOKUP
Toshiba Forum	TOSHIBA
Trademark Research Center($)	TRADERC
TrainNet Forum	TRAINNET

Service/Forum	GO Code
Travel Forum	TRAVSIG
UK Company Library	UKLIB
UK Computing Forum	UKFORUM
UK Historical Stock Pricing	UKPRICE
UK Marketing Library	UKMARKETING
UK News Clips	UKNEWS
UK Newspaper Library	UKPAPERS
UK Sports Clips	UKSPORTS
UK Trademark Library	UKTRADEMARK
UKSHARE Forum	UKSHARE
UNIX Forum	UNIXFORUM
United Press Int'l($)	ENS
Univ of Phoenix(FREE)	UP
UserLand Forum	USERLAND
VAX Forum	VAXFORUM
VISA Advisors	VISA
VISTA Environmental Profiles	VISTA
VL Annual Reports($)	VLANN
VL Quarterly Reports($)	VLQTR
Value Line Financials	COMPAN
Value Line Projections($)	VLFORE
Ventura Software Forum	VENTURA
Vital Stats(FREE)	VS
WORLDSPAN Travelshopper	PARS
WORLDSPAN Travelshopper (CIM)	WORLDCIM
WPMA Forum	WPMA
Walden Computer Books(FREE)	WB
Walter Knoll Florist(FREE)	WK
War Games	WARGAMES
Washington Post($)	ENS
Weather Maps	MAPS
Weather Reports	WEATHER
West Coast Travel	WESTCOAST

Service/Forum	GO Code
What's New	NEW
Windows 3rd Party A Forum	WINAPA
Windows 3rd Party B Forum	WINAPB
Windows 3rd Party C Forum	WINAPC
Windows New Users Forum	WINNEW
Wolfram Research Forum	WOLFRAM
WordPerfect Supp. Group A	WPSGA
WordPerfect Supp. Group B	WPSGB
WordStar Forum	WORDSTAR
Working-From-Home Forum	WORK
YES! Books and Videos(FREE)	YB
You Guessed It!	YGI
ZMAC Edition Ordering	ZMACEDITION
Zenith Data Systems Forum	ZENITH
ZiffNet	ZIFFNET
ZiffNet/Mac	ZMAC

Index

Where?

Read menus, 91-93, 96-99
READ
  commands, 72, 99-101, 147
  options, 97, 130, 242
reading
  CompuServe mail, 130
  forums
    announcements, 81-83
    messages, 68, 100, 130, 259
  mail in Macintosh version, 229
  mail in IBM version, 229
receipts, 136
RECEIVE ALL command, 147
receiving mail, 143-144
Record Incoming Text
    command, 235
recording messages, 125
REDISPLAY (R) command, 182
Reference
  option, 38, 64
  page, 38
  Resources menu, 150-151
rejoining the conference room,
    119
Renew Your Ad ($) option, 219
REPLACE line option, 74, 135
replacing
  lines, 74, 135
  strings, 49
  words, 73
REPLIES info option, 122
Reply button, 249
REPLY
  command, 125
  option, 131
Reply to an Ad option, 219
replying to messages, 91,
    259-260
REREAD this message option,
    131
research services
  accessing, 150
  Academic American
    Encyclopedia, 149-151
  Books in Print, 149
  Business Database Plus, 149
  Computer Library, 149
  Consumer Reports, 149
  Demographics & Government
    Information, 149

Health Database Plus, 149
IQuest, 149-150
Magazine Database Plus, 149
Magill's Survey of Cinema,
    149
Marquis Who's Who, 149
Name/Address/Phone
    Directories, 149
New Car Showroom, 149
Newspaper Library, 150
TV News/Information
    Transcripts, 150
reservations, checking with
    EAASY SABRE, 191-192
RESERVATIONS menu, 191
Restore Previous Selection Set
    option, 201
Retrieve commands, 233-234
returning to forum, 119
REVERSE option, 100
Review options
  results again, 163
  Your Charges, 53
reviewing Navigator sessions,
    249-251
RF (display return fares)
    command, 197
ROF,L (rolling on the floor)
    forum abbreviation, 78
/ROOM conference command,
    120
RS (display return flights)
    command, 197
RSN (real soon now) forum
    abbreviation, 78
Run command, 249

S

/S (initiate schedule request)
    command, 197
S# (display flights for fare
    choice) command, 198
SAVE
  command, 147
  in mailbox option, 131
saving messages, 256
SCAN command, 147
  LIST, 156
  name (access scans), 156
Scan Results menu, 162-163